From
Anxiety
to
Love

From Anxiety to Love

A RADICAL NEW APPROACH FOR LETTING GO OF FEAR AND FINDING LASTING PEACE

CORINNE ZUPKO

FOREWORD BY ROBERT ROSENTHAL, MD

New World Library
Novato, California

New World Library
14 Pamaron Way
Novato, California 94949

Text design by Tona Pearce Myers

Library of Congress Cataloging-in-Publication Data
Names: Zupko, Corinne, [date]– author.
Title: From anxiety to love : a radical new approach for letting go of fear and finding lasting
    peace / Corinne Zupko.
Description: Novato, California : New World Library, [2018] | Includes bibliographical
    references.
Identifiers: LCCN 2017044315 (print) | LCCN 2017051200 (ebook) | ISBN 9781608685066
    (Ebook) | ISBN 9781608685059 (alk. paper)
Subjects: LCSH: Anxiety—Religious aspects. | Peace of mind—Religious aspects. |
    Spiritual life.
Classification: LCC BL627.55 (ebook) | LCC BL627.55 .Z87 2018 (print) | DDC
    152.4/6—dc23
LC record available at https://lccn.loc.gov/2017044315

First printing, February 2018
ISBN 978-1-60868-505-9
Ebook ISBN 978-1-60868-506-6

Printed in Canada on 100% postconsumer-waste recycled paper

New World Library is proud to be a Gold Certified Environmentally Responsible Publisher. Publisher certification awarded by Green Press Initiative. www.greenpressinitiative.org

10   9   8   7   6   5   4   3   2   1

My gratitude and love are eternal...

To my mom and Joseph for remembering the light for me until I could come to remember it for myself. I found peace because of your unwavering dedication to seeking truth.

And to my dear husband, Rob, for being my partner through many lifetimes. I've cherished every moment.

Contents

ᕲᘉᕣ

Part Three: Putting It All Together

Foreword

With an estimated forty million adults currently suffering from anxiety in the United States, it would be fair to say that anxiety is the affliction of our times. This is especially so if we recognize stress as a form of anxiety. More than any other generation of humans, we are saddled today with tasks, responsibilities, and a flood of information well beyond the brain's capacity to manage. If you doubt this, just take a look at your to-do list — then tell me how you feel.

Anxiety is pervasive: the high school senior fretting over college applications; the college senior petrified about finding a job; the young married couple conflicted over whether it's the right time to have a baby; parents worried about their teen's drinking and driving; older workers anticipating layoffs, health issues, and a frugal retirement; and of course seniors, their weeks spent captive to doctors' appointments, hoping to stave off death, terrified that it will sweep down upon them suddenly, yet equally frightened that it will be slow and painful. And these are just the normal forms anxiety takes — the ones we all can relate to. As a psychiatrist, I have treated other, more pathological and far more crippling forms of anxiety, including paralyzing fear over making a simple phone call, heart-racing panic attacks, irrational fears of terrorist bombings, and the delusional conviction that something is wrong with the body that the doctors have repeatedly missed. No matter the form, these symptoms all testify to a sense that life is out of control, fraught with perils seen and unseen about which little can be done.

What's the solution for such pervasive anxiety? Do we simply accept it? Slog through as best we can? Do we give up, drop out, live off the grid? What are our options?

The most common coping strategies for anxiety involve drugs and alcohol. Have a drink, then have another. Get high, pop a pill (illegal or prescription) — and you'll feel better. For a while anyway. But when the buzz wears off, your situation has not changed. In fact, it's likely to feel even worse.

You might try to escape from anxiety by immersing yourself in other kinds of addictive behaviors, seeking out the highs that come from gaming, gambling, sugary foods, sex, or extreme sports, for example. These coping mechanisms all have one thing in common: they look for relief from some source outside the self. As a result, they create dependency — a need, a craving — which in turn gives rise to its own brand of anxiety. What if you run out of your pills? What if your partner catches on to your addiction? And what happens when, inevitably, your addiction of preference no longer satisfies the way it once did? What do you do then?

Instead of searching for a replacement, you could choose to seek out the services of a professional psychotherapist. You might learn (through cognitive behavioral therapy or mindfulness training) to identify those thoughts that habitually stir up anxiety and either replace them with better thoughts or let them go altogether. When the problem is identified as internal — the product of our own thoughts — we are no longer passive victims reacting to circumstances beyond our control. We no longer need to look outside ourselves for a solution. Those pesky thoughts are our responsibility. Once we recognize this, we reclaim the power to change them. Clearly, this is a better approach than drugs or other addictive behaviors, but it is not comprehensive. It does not shield us from life's blows, nor does it help prepare us for the inevitability of death.

The metaphysical thought system taught by the book *A Course in Miracles* (ACIM) offers one of the few solutions to anxiety that is truly comprehensive. It applies to *all* forms of anxiety no matter the circumstances. And it achieves this by guiding us not only to monitor and redirect our thoughts, but to rework from the bottom up our entire sense of who we are and the world we live in.

ACIM tells us that there are only two basic emotions or, more accurately, two states of mind: fear and love. That's it. And they're obviously mutually exclusive. If you're experiencing one, the other is gone. Fear eclipses love, but love banishes fear entirely.

Peace is the companion of love, while anxiety arises from fear. Therefore anxiety (the absence of peace) signals that we are disconnected from love. But ACIM teaches that love is our only reality — who and what we are in truth — and that peace is the natural state of our mind. Therefore, when we're not feeling love and peace, we're not in our right mind — quite literally. We are insane. Welcome to the world!

According to ACIM, then, the anxiety we all feel is inevitable. It will plague us so long as we believe ourselves to be something we're not: separate individuals, each different, housed in vulnerable physical bodies, moving through an uncaring world over which we have little control, and subject to the whims and depredations of time. If your true self is not a body, but spirit, then what harm can come to you? And if your true abode is not the world of linear time, where past and future overhang that slim, ungraspable instant that is *now*, then what is there to be anxious about? Anxiety is nothing more than fear projected into the future: fear about what *might* occur at some future time. Love is lived only in present tense.

In *From Anxiety to Love*, psychotherapist Corinne Zupko takes the key principles of *A Course in Miracles* and adapts them in a user-friendly way to counter and ultimately eradicate anxiety. Corinne writes both as a professional and as someone who has herself confronted severe anxiety. She shares examples of her own struggles in a manner that's moving, insightful, and humorous in order to demonstrate how she learned to apply ACIM to her life and become more peaceful.

However, this book is not only for motivated anxiety sufferers. Veteran students of ACIM should also find it helpful. The lessons and quotations may offer little that's new. It is Corinne's dedication to putting those lessons into practice, as well as her emphasis on cultivating a *willingness* to change rather than forcing change prematurely, that makes this book a worthwhile adjunct to ACIM study.

Although it is full of helpful meditations, affirmations, and practices, please do not mistake *From Anxiety to Love* for just another self-help book or power-of-positive-thinking instruction manual. Because it rests on the principles of ACIM, it leads the reader into a radical system of not just thought change, but mind change. If we are insane and the world is our asylum, then consider this book a key to escape and a path to sanity. If we are trapped in turbulent dreams, this is the soft whisper and gentle caress that call us to awaken.

You may not believe all this book promises. But as ACIM itself states, you don't have to *believe* any of it. You just need to try it out. Give it a chance. Take it for a test drive. Practice the exercises. Let the results themselves convince you. What do you have to lose, but your fear?

— Robert Rosenthal, MD,
board-certified psychiatrist and
author of *From Never-Mind to Ever-Mind*
and *From Plagues to Miracles*

Prologue

⤷⤶

At 3 AM, it's pitch-black in my college dormitory room when I'm awakened by a punch in the gut from a flood of stress hormones. My heart starts racing, I break out in a sweat, and my stomach feels like it's flipped over and is dropping to my knees. I jolt upright because I can't breathe. I'm certain I'm about to die. Pure terror floods my veins.

Nearly blinded by the dark, I climb down the ladder of my bunk bed, hoping not to wake my roommate. I grab the phone, stretching the wire out the door so I can escape to the bathroom of my suite. My body is shaking uncontrollably; it's hard to control my arms and legs. I sit on the cold tile floor, finding that my tears make it even harder to breathe.

Unsteadily I dial my home number. My mom picks up the phone, thank God.

"Mom?"

"Corinne? What's the matter?"

"Mom…I don't know what's happening to me….I'm shaking….I — I can't breathe."

"Where are you? Are you sitting down?"

"Yes. I'm on my bathroom floor."

"Good. All right now, try and just breathe in a little."

There is silence while my mom waits. When I speak again, my voice is tight, high-pitched, strained.

"Mom, my body is shaking.... I can hardly walk..."

"Corinne, are you sick? Do you have a temperature?"

"It feels like a heart attack.... My heart is racing, and I'm terrified."

"You're going to be fine, Corinne. Your heart is healthy. Did something happen?"

My mom's response calms me a little so I can think. "A student died yesterday. I'm so scared I'm going to die next.... I've never felt so terrified before."

"Okay, it's okay. Everything is going to be all right. You might be having an anxiety attack. Talk to me."

"I'm sorry I woke you up." The tears start flowing again. "I can't breathe..."

"It's okay, Corinne.... Take a deep breath.... Take your time; tell me what happened."

I breathe in and out, once. "A student died yesterday morning of meningitis. He was at a party the night before he died, and he's dead now. He was fine at the party. I'm terrified that this is going to happen to me."

"You're safe, Corinne. Keep breathing. Tell me more."

"I feel like I'm going to die. It feels like I'm seeing and hearing through a tunnel. I can't stop shaking. I'm afraid my suite mates are going to wake up and find me here."

"Okay, take some deep breaths with me. Remember the relaxation technique you learned when you were little? We're going to practice this now. Breathe with me. Let's take a breath in...and out..."

We breathe together. I'm getting more air, but my body and legs continue to tremble violently on the cold bathroom tiles. "Mom, I am afraid I'm not going to come out of this. The terror...the shaking....They're not stopping."

"It's going to subside, Corinne. Do you want to come home?"

Actually, I'd love to go home right now; *home* sounds so safe. But the semester is nearly over. "I can't," I sigh. "I have a final exam in the morning." Determination wells up in me: *I will not let anxiety get in the way of my education.*

"Then we'll stay on the phone as long as we need to."

"Thank you, Mom!" Her support helps, but the flood of terror doesn't subside.

"Keep talking to me, Corinne. Tell me what you're afraid of."

"I'm afraid of death. I'm afraid of dying. I'm afraid *you're* going to die. I'm afraid of getting sick. Of suffering....Death seems like that's the only guarantee in this world. I'm so full of terror. People say that God is love, but...how can a loving God create things that die?"

I can't tell if I'm making any sense.

"Corinne, it's good that you're talking about this. Looking at your fears means that they won't have as much power over you. We'll keep talking about this...and how would you feel about getting connected with a counselor, too?"

"I'm totally open to that....I'll try anything that can help me."

"We were meant to talk tonight, honey. I know this because somehow I heard the phone ring...you know how I sleep in a fortress!"

I chuckle through my tears, visualizing how my mom sleeps with earplugs and a white noise maker, anything to blot out noise.

"Something guided me to wake up and hear the phone. We need to trust that. Trust that we're going to find a way to get you through this."

0097924680

"Okay, I will." My declaration of trust brings about a glimmer of love in my heart. My hope is increasing, and my body is calming.

"Corinne, I know you haven't wanted to talk about this before, but that book I study, *A Course in Miracles*, has exercises in it that might be really helpful for you. It's all about learning how to undo fear."

Guilt flashes through my mind as I remember the times in the past that my mom tried to talk to me about the Course. With teenage defiance, I would put my hands over my ears and exclaim, "Speak to me in *English* like you used to! I'm not interested in this spiritual stuff!" But now I'm desperate.

"I'll try anything, Mom.... That sounds good."

"We're going to get you through this. You're going to be okay. We're going to find help for you."

Our conversation continues for a while, until I am calm enough to climb back into my bunk bed, taking my headphones and CD player. I fall asleep listening to soothing music. That turns out to be the only way I'll be able to fall asleep for the next six months.

My mom and I agreed that this episode meant I was beginning to face the anxiety that had been building within me since I was a baby. I knew there had to be a way through it, and I was determined to find it. Nothing was going to stop me in my search for peace, even though there were many times when I doubted I'd ever find it.

Introduction

❧

*I*f you have ever had a panic attack, you know how hard the feeling is to describe to someone who has never had one. It is pure inner hell. On the high end of the anxiety spectrum, where I spent a large part of my life, are panic attacks, debilitating fear, and free-floating anxiety. On the low end of the spectrum are the normal fears and anxieties that occasionally visit all of us. This book is about how to work with your anxiety, regardless of where it falls along this spectrum.

My anxiety journey was one of the worst, most terrifying experiences of my life. Yet once I allowed it to become my greatest teacher, it also became one of the best. My anxiety brought me to greater inner peace than I ever thought I could experience, and for that, I'm incredibly grateful. I hope this book will help you be grateful for your anxiety, too, because anxiety is a call to awakening and can start you on a pathway toward love and inner peace.

Every experience you have can serve one of two purposes — and you get to choose which. It can help you awaken to the peace that is already in you, or it can help you stay unaware of this peace. In this world, we are conditioned to choose the latter. This book will help you choose to wake up to peace.

In these pages, I describe the process I used to work myself out of terror and into an anxiety-free life. And by working that process, I'm now doing things I never thought I would be capable of: taking plane trips fearlessly, and without medications, by myself; speaking confidently in front of large audiences; traveling into New York City by myself without feeling completely overwhelmed; sleeping like a baby instead of having horrible insomnia; and awakening without early-morning anxiety. If I can experience such radical changes in my life, so can you.

The spiritual practice that helped me out of anxiety is called *A Course in Miracles*.* The Course is a system of loosening our fixed, fearful perceptions so we can rediscover the peace that is already within us. At first you may find this new system of thought hard to follow, but don't worry about it. If the Course is your path to healing, it will gradually begin to make sense as you become willing to understand it. You do not have to believe in it, but if you test its concepts, the results will speak for themselves. My approach in this book is just one way of exploring the deep teachings of the Course and is based on my interpretation and experience of its principles. I hope it will help you learn to listen directly to your Inner Therapist, which is the part of your mind that helps you to heal. For consistency, I use the term *Inner Therapist* throughout this book, but feel free to call it whatever you'd like: *Inner Teacher*, *Inner Guide*, *Holy Spirit*, and *Higher Mind* are common ways of referring to the part of your mind that recognizes your eternal reality.

Together we'll discover new ways to look at the world and

---

* Foundation for Inner Peace, *A Course in Miracles: Combined Volume*, 3rd. ed. (Mill Valley, CA: Foundation for Inner Peace, 2007). Please see the appendix for an explanation of the annotation system used in the citations.

practical strategies to restore your awareness of peace. In part 1, we explore our collective descent into anxiety. In part 2, we work through the healing steps and perception shifts that can help us ascend out of anxiety. In part 3, we put it all together and examine practical techniques for dealing with the many ways that anxiety shows up in life.

In this book I talk about God. We have a lot of baggage attached to this word, because human beings have used God to justify many unloving and atrocious acts. When I use the word *God*, please know that I am not referring to a dude with a white beard who sits upstairs and orchestrates things down here. God has no gender.* I am referring to an all-encompassing Divine Love that is *only* loving and is incapable of causing pain. It is part of us and not outside ourselves. I also refer to it as *our Source, Oneness,* and *Love.* These words are capitalized as a reminder that I am referring to God. I also capitalize additional terms when I am referring to concepts beyond this world of form.

In addition, *miracles* aren't big, magical events; rather, they can occur at any moment in the day if we allow them to. Miracles can be defined in two different but interrelated ways. According to *A Course in Miracles,* "miracles are expressions of love" (ACIM T-1.I.35); but they are also shifts in perception. This book emphasizes the latter definition, because when we are caught in fear, we must learn to shift our perception. These shifts were essential to me in finding relief from debilitating anxiety. This new definition of miracles may seem less exciting, but there is nothing more

---

* In some quotations from *A Course in Miracles,* masculine pronouns are used to describe God and the Holy Spirit (which I refer to as our Inner Therapist). Although I avoid masculine pronouns in this book, I have left these Course quotes in their original form. The Holy Spirit, your Inner Therapist, is beyond male or female, but you can imagine it as male, female, or gender-neutral, as you like.

satisfying than coming to recognize your eternal nature, which cannot change, grow old, or experience anxiety.

If you use this book with an open mind and adopt an attitude of "I don't know" rather than clinging to what you think you already know, you will create space for new insights to come to you. Willingness to learn new ideas is key, and any voice that tells you you'll never succeed is not your real voice. And if this message resonates with you, I highly recommend getting a copy of *A Course in Miracles* and diving in. It's a life-changing pathway that continues to deepen my awareness of peace in ways I could not previously comprehend.

Inner peace is not an event: it's a process. It's not something we attain once and keep forever, but rather an experience that continues to deepen to the degree to which you're willing to get out of the way and allow peace to move through you. I promise that you are worth the effort. I'm imagining that we're holding hands in our shared commitment to undoing anxiety. Let's do this.

PART ONE

∽◦∽

The Descent
into
Anxiety

CHAPTER ONE

A New Way of Seeing the World

Be still, and lay aside all thoughts of what you are and
what God is; all concepts you have learned about the world;
all images you hold about yourself.

A Course in Miracles, W-pI.189.7:1

We hold many false perceptions in our mind. These false perceptions *are purposeful blocks to our peace of mind.* Paradoxical though it may seem, we hold on to mistaken ways of seeing *because* they make us unhappy. We're all addicted, to some degree, to being afraid and miserable. But we're not usually aware of this addiction, and that's what can make the world seem cruel or scary. We think our problems or enemies are "out there" in the world, but in fact they're mostly within our own habitual, unproductive ways of seeing. And they are hard to undo without extraordinary help.

Fortunately, you have an effective way to change your ways of seeing, and that is through your Inner Therapist. What I call the *Inner Therapist* is also known as the *Holy Spirit*, your *Higher Mind*, or your *Inner Teacher*. You can call it whatever you like. I capitalize terms like these when I am referring to concepts beyond this world of form. Your Inner Therapist is *not* separate from or external to you, but it is outside fear.

Our Inner Therapist holds the key to inner peace because it knows what really makes us happy. It is that small, quiet Voice inside that always tells us that we are loved, that we are safe, and that we have done nothing wrong. It does not analyze or judge us: it simply sees our inner light. You won't hear this Voice if you are regretting the past or worrying about the future; your Inner Therapist is always heard in the present moment. The feeling of connection with your Inner Therapist is deeply gratifying and enormously comforting. It engenders pure joy. It is like coming home. But this happy, carefree childhood feeling can be easily drowned out by busyness, worry, and all the distractions of the world. When you learn to stay consistently in touch with your Inner Therapist, however, you can literally be a miracle worker.

My perspective on healing anxiety through the Inner Therapist is chiefly inspired by *A Course in Miracles*, which is a unique psychospiritual system for changing the way we look at the world. Diving into the Course completely and wholeheartedly was my way out of an internal hell. For me, accepting its radical view of our existence was the key to overcoming chronic anxiety. I needed an explanation of a crazy world that made no sense to me. I needed another way to look at everything, because the way I was seeing constantly frightened me. *A Course in Miracles* turned everything in my world on its head — and then answered every big question I'd ever had in a completely new way.

Who Are We Really?

You are not who you think you are — and this is glorious news. You are not your fear, your anxiety, or your worry. You may feel that these things define you, because they are really good at capturing and overpowering your attention. That is their purpose. But the fearful, freaked-out, anxious you is not the true you, despite how compellingly real that fear and anxiety seem. What you really are is way more awesome. I promise.

If, like me, you have struggled with deep anxiety about death, sickness, and suffering, I've got good news for you. What you really are is love, and love only. Your true nature actually exists in an eternal state, a creative state in which you are entirely happy and at peace. You cannot die; you cannot become sick; you exist forever; and you will know yourself even after this body is laid aside. You've probably heard teachings like this before. But we're going to work toward experiencing the truth of these words, for it's the experience of these teachings that provides relief from anxiety.

You have forgotten the eternal love that you are made of because right now you believe you are confined in a body, in a particular time and place. But, in fact, *you are a pure, Loving Mind.* This Loving Mind exists independently of your ego personality and also of the "mind" generated by your brain. Your reality is actually abstract, not physical. You are not your body. Yes, you do *seem* to have a body right now, just like you have clothes — but everyone knows that their clothes aren't their real selves. The clothes are just something useful to keep us warm and protected, and perhaps to express our personalities.

The idea of existing beyond your body may be hard to grasp or even imagine at first, because we are literally asleep to it most of the time. We have forgotten our existence in eternity and mistakenly think that the world we see is our home. I've always gained comfort from this Course quote, which helps me begin to understand a world that is very different from the one we see:

Sit quietly and look upon the world you see, and tell yourself: "The real world is not like this. It has no buildings and there are no streets where people walk alone and separate. There are no stores where people buy an endless list of things they do not need. It is not lit with artificial light, and night comes not upon it. There is no day that brightens and grows dim. There is no loss. Nothing is there but shines, and shines forever." (ACIM T-13.VII.1:1–6)

So in truth, we're perfectly at peace. We are eternal, united in joy, equally loved and loving; we shine forever.

Does eternal bliss sound good to you? Or does it sound like cosmic oatmeal, bland and boring? I can certainly understand if you're thinking, "Eternal bliss sounds lovely, but too lofty. Get real! I feel anything but peaceful, happy, or loving. And also, I have a cold." Before we can see the world in a new way that promotes peace, we need to explore the nature of this seemingly real, pessimistic, fearful voice in our minds, which we are going to call *the ego*.

Down the Ego Rabbit Hole

Down, down, down. Would the fall never come to an end?
"I wonder how many miles I've fallen by this time?"
she said aloud. "I must be getting somewhere near the
centre of the earth. . . . I wonder if I shall fall right through
the earth! How funny it'll seem to come out among the
people that walk with their heads downward!"

Lewis Carroll, *Alice's Adventures in Wonderland*

The ego is a belief in your mind that you are a body with a personality instead of an eternal being. It is a belief or idea that you are separate from God. The ego turns our perception upside down because it is a thought system that expresses traits that are the opposite of God. If God is eternal life, the ego believes in death. If God is unconditional love, the ego is an expert at judgment and giving love only to those it deems worthy. If God is perfect harmlessness, the ego calls forth pain. If God sees only what is true, the ego sees only what is false.

The ego may seem like a big deal, but it's just a "tiny, mad idea" that we have accepted into our minds (ACIM T-27.VIII.6:2). It's a fearful, false voice that wants to keep us identified with a small sense of self.

Do you ever get a really silly idea that you just can't let go of? Even if you suspect it's all wrong, you might take it seriously for a long time. For example, my family once lived in a rental house that had an inground pool, which was freezing cold. Obsessed with the desire to get his kids swimming, my dad got the idea that he could boil four pots of water at a time on our electric kitchen stove and dump the boiling water into the forty-thousand-gallon pool to raise the temperature. Even at the age of ten, I knew this wouldn't work. But he believed it would, and raced to boil his next batch of water after dumping one batch into the pool. Only after repeated failures to raise the water temperature did he finally look for another way. He discovered solar panels on the roof of the house that could be rigged to warm the pool water.

The ego is a silly thought that we have chosen to take seriously. Believing in it plays a huge role in contributing to anxiety. Until we see how the belief in ego actually causes unhappiness, we won't be inclined to let go of it. In my quest to find freedom from the ego, I sought answers to some big existential questions that had plagued me for years. One big question is, Why did I accept the ego into my mind in the first place? The answer is *specialness*.

Our Loving Source doesn't know specialness. Everything in

Love's eyes is equally special. This means that no one is special
— an idea that is almost incomprehensible on this earthly plane,
where our specialness is literally equal to our survival.

While we (the Children of God) are really still at home in Love,
some of us decide that we want to call the shots, be cooler than the
bunch, different from the rest — and we certainly want to write our
own script of life, rather than just exist in the perfection that was
given to us. Love, being One and only knowing Oneness, cannot
give us the specialness we so vehemently desire. You could say that,
being children, we have a special case of the "terrible twos": oneness, unity, and infinite love just aren't good enough for us because
we want to experience two-ness, also called *duality*. This duality
sounds like our own personal, delightful Disneyland.

So, to get the specialness that Love can't give us, we decide to
blow off Love. By turning our back on our Loving Source of Oneness, we believe we can find, maintain, and enhance our specialness.
We grab onto our "tiny, mad idea" of specialness and take it so seriously that we end up getting lost in it and can no longer remember being in constant, loving communication with our Source. We
are mesmerized by our dream of duality and individuality, but that
dream is often a nightmare. This is an error we make not just once
but perpetually, as we choose to keep dreaming of a substitute for
Oneness. Because this initial choice was not made on a conscious
individual level, we have no memory of it. However, we can easily
see evidence of our desire for specialness in our lives.

ACTIVITY: IDENTIFYING SPECIALNESS

In working with your Inner Therapist, honesty is key.
Let's acknowledge our sense of specialness. List ways
you want to be special. For instance, maybe you want

to have a prestigious job, to be recognized for a notable achievement, to live in a highly desirable location, or to stand out in a crowd for your great sense of humor or the way you dress. List all of the ways you would love to be special. Remember, we *all* do this, so there is no reason to feel guilty. Specialness is in the fabric of our existence on this earthly plane. Look without judgment at each of the ways you'd like to be special, and give yourself a pat on the back for being honest. You're setting yourself up for good work with your Inner Therapist.

Next, let's look at another of my big questions: How did we end up in this world? The answer here is likely different from anything you've heard (so keep your mind open), but it explains a core source of anxiety: guilt.

When we chose to turn away from Love to claim special-ness, that choice had some nasty side effects. Just as a puppy curls its tail between its legs when it perceives it has done something wrong, we feel massive guilt for turning our back on our Loving Source. Right on the heels of this extreme guilt, we become fearful that our Loving Source will get angry and punish us for turning away. This cannot actually happen, because God is Love, and Love only. God is incapable of being anything other than loving. But we accept the idea of guilt into part of our Loving Mind.

Can you think of an example from your childhood where you did something that ended up hurting your parents' feelings? I sure can. When I was thirteen years old, I was once so angry with my mother that I hid in my bedroom closet and didn't answer her calls for over thirty minutes. Frantic to find me, she went outside to check if I was on my dad's boat or had fallen into the river. As she stepped onto the boat, she slipped and severely bruised her leg. I felt guilty not only for causing her emotional distress but also for causing her to get physically hurt. I cried for days and never did anything like that again.

If you can connect with my sense of guilt for hurting my mom, imagine increasing this guilt exponentially by thinking that we have deeply hurt God by choosing to turn our backs on our Source *and* that God is mad at us for it. Sounds like a great reason to be anxious, right? Unconscious guilt from our belief that we have cut ourselves off from God is a huge source of anxiety. But instead of getting caught forever in this unconscious guilt, we can learn to see it differently and allow it to be healed. We'll explore how to do that in part 2 of this book. For now, let's do a simple experiment in seeing differently.

ACTIVITY:
CHANGING THE WAY WE SEE OURSELVES

We hold many images about ourselves. Some of these images are roles that we play in life (e.g., parent, spouse, child, friend, activist), jobs we hold (teacher, spiritual teacher, employee, executive), ideas about our talents or abilities (creative, analytical, untalented, ingenious), and ideas about our bodies or mind states (attractive, not attractive enough, thin, heavy-set, anxious, depressed, emotional).

Take a moment to write down as many images as you can think of that you hold about yourself. What are some roles that you play in life? What profession do you identify with? What are your abilities? How do you view your body? Your state of mind? Some of these images may be "positive" images, and some may be "negative."

Do you feel that you would be happier if some of these images were different? Write down what images you might want to change in order to be happy.

All of these images, whether or not they accurately describe you, or whether or not they make you happy, are aspects of the small self. Your small self (with a low-ercase *s*) is the ego. It is your belief in a body that is separate from Love, and its identity is based on roles that are subject to change. For instance, all the images of yourself that you have just listed are transient. They can change with time or circumstances.

Your capital-S Self is very different. It does not change with time: it remains in a constant state of pure joy. It is pure Spirit, not limited to a body, and not subject to sickness, aging, or death. This is the Self you once knew and have forgotten about. You want to come to know this Self again because it is always at peace. Anxiety cannot exist in your changeless Self.

To recognize your changelessness and to begin to remember your Self, look at your responses to this exercise and remind yourself that you want the experience of being happy and at peace, and that true happiness comes from a place in your mind beyond all images. Ask yourself, "Am I willing to release all of these ideas about myself in order to remember something even greater lies within me? Am I willing to even release the images that I think will make me happy?" Take a deep breath, and be willing to release all of these ideas about yourself. You don't have to actually release them — you just have to be *willing* to. Say to yourself, "I am willing to see myself differently. I am willing to accept a miracle and to remember my Self." This willingness is the key to doing good work with your Inner Therapist.

This chapter has explored some new ways of seeing yourself, the fearful voice in your mind (ego), its quest for specialness, and the rise of guilt, and it has touched on the idea that this world may not be our true home. I give you full permission to not buy any of it! But just as you are willing to release your perceptions of yourself, can you also be willing to be open to a new way of seeing the world — not through the ego but through the eyes of our loving Inner Therapist? You don't have to believe a thing I say. Just try out some of the practices and let the results speak for themselves.

Questions for Reflection

1. Have you ever realized that you were stuck in unproductive or mistaken perceptions about yourself? What were the most important ones, and how did life change when you were able to let them go?
2. Have you ever felt that there is something really off about your idea of yourself — that you might have your "self" all wrong?
3. Do you sometimes feel guilty or afraid for no apparent reason?

CHAPTER TWO

Awakening from a Not-So-Sweet Dream

~ை~

The Bible says that a deep sleep fell upon Adam,
and nowhere is there reference to his waking up.
The world has not yet experienced any comprehensive
reawakening or rebirth.

A Course in Miracles, T-2.I.3:6–7

I have been anxious most of my life. When I was around one
year old, my mom went through a trauma and was whisked
away for a weeklong stay in the hospital. On her return, I rejected her, angry that she had left me. After we rebonded, she was
"blessed" with a child with severe separation anxiety; I screamed
at the top of my lungs whenever she left my sight.

Although a lot of my later childhood anxiety was rooted
in normal childhood fears — worry that I might lose my parents, shame about being made fun of in school — I also fixated
on weird things that I never told anyone about. When I was in
kindergarten, I obsessively worried that I was pregnant because I
liked a boy. In the second grade, I had a phobia about flushing the
toilet because I was afraid it would overflow. Not long after that,

I developed a fear of going to restaurants because I was afraid of overeating and then becoming nauseated. I felt panicky if left alone with my grandfather because I was afraid he would die in front of me. In middle school, I thought every belly pain meant I had appendicitis. Because of our family's financial stresses, I also worried intensely that we might lose our house. By the age of twelve, I had an ulcer.

Although I had been to counseling as a child, my mother knew that eventually I would have to come face to face with the terror and fears of loss I carried into adulthood. She wanted any decision about medication to be mine; she understood that she could not fix my problems for me. I needed to find coping tools and answers for myself.

So when I found myself on the bathroom floor that night in college, fearing my own death, I realized I was coming face to face with the terror within. The anxiety was like a leech, sucking any semblance of inner peace out of me, swelling into a monster. I felt powerless to control it, and it seemed that it would never leave me.

About forty million Americans suffer from anxiety disorders. I knew I was among them, but it would be a while before I recognized that membership in this club was a profound existential issue. I was really in a nightmare club that *everyone* has joined.

How do we wake up from this nightmare of anxiety? First, we have to recognize that it *is* a nightmare. And I'm speaking literally, not figuratively. One of the most helpful things I've learned from *A Course in Miracles* is to look at the world as if it is all a dream. This dream is playing out in an unconscious part of our mind, which I call the Child Mind, for we're Children in the Mind of God. Think of it this way: The Mind of God created a Child Mind, which comprises many Children. Although the Child Mind remains at home in the Love of God, part of it has fallen asleep and is dreaming of a world of separate bodies. These sleeping Children are you and me.

If your head is spinning, take a deep breath and keep reading!

Think for a moment about how real your dreams feel when you're sleeping. I used to have a recurring dream of being at college, suddenly realizing I was sitting on a toilet in the middle of the cafeteria with my pants around my ankles, and everyone could see me. I can still recall how mortified I felt, only to wake up and realize with a huge sigh of relief that it was only a dream. It turned out I had been safe in my bed the whole time.

The sleeping part of our Child Mind is still safe in bed. It has not left its home in Love, and it still has the power of God in it. But it chooses to believe in the ego, and thus it dreams a dream of bodies, of a material world of time and space, a realm of separation and of death. These are the "witnesses" of the ego, the evidence it gives you to convince you that this world is your reality (ACIM W-pI.161.10:4). These are also our "waking dreams" (ACIM T-18.II.5:13). According to this perspective, the world we all see is a manifestation, a vivid dream, of a powerful mind that is asleep. Just as our sleeping dreams feel real, so does this waking dream of the world. This is because we have misused the power of God to make ourselves forget that we are the Children of God.

At first, it might seem anxiety provoking to think of the world as a dream. But the "you" that transcends your body is true and real. You will always know your Self, and your reality is not limited to your senses. If you've ever had a feeling of connection to something "greater than yourself" or a sense of being lifted above the chaos of daily life, you've already experienced this awareness. Your Inner Therapist can help you remember your real being, which you have forgotten through your identification with your body. Imagine the sense of safety and calm you can have walking around in this world knowing that nothing can hurt or change who you really are. Anxiety cannot exist in the face of this knowledge. This is what we're working toward. But to get there, we have to look further at our choice to believe in our ego identity, because its witnesses are very compelling!

The sleeping part of our Child Mind, our daily sense of a separated self or ego identity, is terrified that it is going to get into trouble for turning its back on God. It is plagued by unconscious fear and guilt. Those feelings soon become intolerable, especially when we can dimly remember that our Child Mind is actually owned by Love. So then we end up with *projection*.

Spitting Out Our Fear and Guilt

I once witnessed a child who was projectile vomiting. This kid's belly said, "Out you go!" to milk and hurled it across the room, splattering white chunks everywhere — the kind of sight that's really hard to unsee. Like this lactose-intolerant child, the sleeping part of our Child Mind has to get rid of the intolerable fear and guilt it feels for cherishing the dreamworld of specialness and separation. Yet by projecting massive fear and guilt outward, we actually reinforce our sense of separation, because now there is meaning to the idea of "out there," which makes no sense in Oneness. Projection, in a sense, is like mental vomiting. Now the fear and guilt *seem* to be outside our mind, and the sense of relief we feel from apparently expelling them ensures that we can continue on our merry way down the path of separation from our Loving Source.

"Projection makes perception," the Course reminds us (ACIM T-13.V.3:5). Projection literally gives us something to perceive, and usually we don't realize that we are perceiving not *facts*, but our own prejudiced interpretations. For example, I dislike cold weather. In winter, when I see the squirrels and deer outside, I think, "Those animals must be freezing. I'll bet they hate the winter!" But animals live outside and adapt to cold temperatures; they're not freezing. Their supposed dislike of the cold is entirely in my mind, but I project that thought outward, creating the perception that the deer and squirrels feel the same way I do. In reality, they wouldn't wear wool sweaters even if I were to knit some for them.

And so it goes at every moment, on scales large and small. What is inside gets projected outside and makes the external world we see. "The mind is very powerful, and never loses its creative force," says the Course. "It never sleeps. Every instant it is creating. It is hard to recognize that thought and belief combine into a power surge that can literally move mountains" (ACIM T-2.VI.9:5–8).

ACTIVITY: IDENTIFYING YOUR PROJECTIONS

We don't project fear and guilt only once as a Child Mind, but rather we continue to project our beliefs all the time. These projections act as a barrier to the peace awaiting us within. Becoming aware of some of your projections is the first step in allowing them to be undone. A key indicator of a projection is that there is a "story" you're telling yourself about the situation, a story that may or may not be true.

For instance, suppose your boss is in a bad mood, and you immediately decide you must have done something wrong. The projection is your own fear projected onto your boss. Or maybe, after watching a violent movie, you feel unsafe walking outside when you didn't before.

Write down every projection you can think of that occurred today (again without judgment).

As we get better at identifying our projections, we begin to understand how much what we see is shaped by our interpretations. Taking responsibility for our projections is a key to working with our Inner Therapist to remember the truth of who we are.

It can be a challenge to remember your eternal reality when the outside world is so convincingly real. The world's purpose is to "prove" that you are a separate body and can be hurt; that death is real and always threatening; that we must suffer to grow. Yet all these anxieties are simply the effects of projection. We see scary things because scary thoughts are in our mind.

Experiencing the world through the fearful projection of the sleeping part of the Child Mind is like visiting a warped theme park and believing it is real. We exchange eternal Oneness for the temporary roller coaster of being born, growing old, and dying. We exchange the peace of God for a dream of chaos, a peaceful Self-knowledge for the twisted fun house of the ego, and infinite life for sickness and death. Our curiosity to experience what it was like to be special and separate from Love (God) has placed us in a world that can be vicious at times.

Take nature. I love it so much, yet it can be so cruel. It has always seemed insane to me that living things have to kill other living things to survive. I used to sob during nature programs that showed animals hunting other animals. Even eating only plants doesn't get us off the hook: studies show that plants go on the defensive when they perceive an attack (i.e., when we harvest them). I recently started growing a lot of my own veggies, but I am learning that even organic gardening involves a lot of killing: I must keep the cabbage worms from eating my kale by collecting them and squishing them, or spraying them with soapy water and watching them wither in pain and die. Yuck.

Seen through the ego's eyes, this world can be a harsh place, full of suffering, interspersed with fragments of seeming beauty. Adults, children, and babies are susceptible to diseases and death. Everything we see will one day perish. Even the continents beneath our feet are shifting and changing. Nothing is stable here. The situation is pretty bleak.

Or is it?

Welcome to Nonduality

Thank goodness there is another way to see the world. We can wake up from the nightmare here and now by adopting the perspective of nonduality. In this view there is only one reality, and the one we see around us ain't it. Only Love is true: the rest is a dream created not by God out of Love, but instead by the sleeping part of our Child Mind as a hiding place from Love. Our ego's crazed thinking is that if we hide out here and forget who we are, maybe we'll avoid being punished for blowing off God.

This unique perspective is like Neo in *The Matrix* choosing to take the red pill, thus gaining a new awareness of what is real. We've been terribly mistaken in our perception of reality. It turns out there is nothing to be afraid of here. If you feel the ego flaring up with fear at the idea that the world isn't our reality, take note: *it is only the ego that's afraid*. Now you have the opportunity to set the cornerstone of a new foundation of inner peace, rather than continuing to rely on a termite-infested foundation of anxiety.

"You do not want the world. The only thing of value in it is whatever part of it you look upon with love. This gives it the only reality it will ever have" (ACIM T-12.VI.3:1–3). On reading this Course quote, you might disagree with the idea of not wanting the world. "What about the things I love in the world? The beach? The mountains? Animals? My children? Artwork or a beautiful sunset? I *do* want these things!"

The good news is that we give up *nothing* in the process of awakening from anxiety to love. The only thing we lose is fear. We're simply learning to see through a new set of lenses, or a change of mind. The beauty and love we see around us derive from the Love of God that is pouring through us and lighting up these forms. As we begin to wake up, this extension of love happens more frequently, not less.

When people first encounter the notion of the world's unreality, they often feel that they must deny or *detach* themselves from it. This isn't really possible. We might be able to tell ourselves, "This world isn't real," but guess what: we still believe that it is entirely real. I'm really into nonduality, but if a speeding truck is heading straight for me, I'm going to get out of the way. *We made this world real for ourselves*, and we love what we've made. We love the self-concepts we've made, we love the world we've made, and we're hell-bent on not letting go of any of it while gamely hoping it will all work out somehow.

We have to recognize and own up to this part of ourselves that *wants* to be a body, beleaguered and separate from Love, because being honest about this plays an important role in healing anxiety.

ACTIVITY:
FINDING THE BENEFITS OF NEGATIVE STATES

We don't choose fear and guilt just once: we hang on to negative states all the time. Try this idea: there is a positive payoff for every negative state. Identify one unwanted aspect of your life that you would like to change. It may be a behavior (like getting into constant arguments), a mind state (like anxiety), or a body state (like sickness). With extreme self-honesty and *no* judgment, write out any and every positive payoff to that behavior that you can think of. What do you get out of it? What is the benefit to you? Do you get attention? Sympathy? Seeming love? Is it an excuse for getting people to leave you alone? It can be surprising to see the positive outcomes that we unconsciously seek from negative situations.

The ego prefers to keep all of this hidden, so kudos to you for being willing to look at it. Darkness is undone by bringing it to the light. The payoff of guilt and fear is the experience of a separate self, which we seek because it makes us feel special and lets us live a life that is seemingly independent from our Source. As we learn how to change our minds and see the world, our guilt, and our anxiety from a different perspective, we gain more of a sense of our Self, and the *only* thing we lose is pain.

We can change the way we see because we have a constant, sure, and unwavering connection to our Loving Source, even in the midst of the everyday world. We didn't really separate from our Source; we just wholeheartedly *believe* that we did. Our connection is what the Course calls the Holy Spirit and what I call your Inner Therapist. Every instant that we entertain the "tiny, mad idea" that we can exist separately from the Love of God as egos, our Inner Therapist is there to remind us that we *don't* have to be permanently lost in the dream.

Now we can answer my remaining big existential question: "Why are we here?" From the perspective of the ego, we are here to forget who we really are. From the perspective of our Inner Therapist, we are here to *remember* who we truly are.

As we begin to remember, we overcome anxiety. Right now we are identified with dream figures in the sleeping part of our Child Mind, believing we are our ego identities in these bodies, and in this world. Working with our Inner Therapist, we begin a gentle process of waking the sleeping part of our Child Mind to the awareness that it never left its Loving Source and that it is *not happy* being separate from our Source. We are also reassured that our Source isn't mad at us, and we are *not* guilty. As we come to this knowledge, anxiety falls away.

Ideas and Their Source

Remember how I said projection is like mental vomiting? Although throwing up can temporarily solve the problem of a

baby's aversion to milk, it doesn't work so well with our problem
of inner guilt and fear. By projecting the fear and guilt outward,
the sleeping Child Mind does not actually get rid of it. This is because "ideas leave not their source" (ACIM T-26.VII.4:7).

Here's an analogy. One summer I learned that residents of a
nearby town were experiencing electric shocks in their inground
swimming pools. Ouch! Apparently the electricity was traveling
through the ground, trying to find its way back home to the electric company's generating station. The article went on to explain
that electricity always seeks to return to its source to complete its
circuit. Our ideas are similar to electricity: they remain connected
to their source even if they stray. They always remain connected to
the mind that thought them, even if that mind chooses to forget
them.

If ideas do not leave their source, then the attempt to project our fear and guilt outward simply cannot work. The worldly
threats we constantly defend ourselves against — sickness, depri-
vation, conflict — are actually projections that originate in the
sleeping part of our Child Mind and have not left their Source. To
heal them, we have to look into the mind. But if we instead just try
to defend ourselves against them, the need for defenses "proves"
to us that they must be real, and we won't look to the place where
real healing lies. It is a perfect setup to keep us from waking up
and seeing that the cause of suffering is actually within our mind.

Although it may seem like there are a lot of worldly threats
that we need to watch out for, we can wake up in an instant, because we have not left our Source. You and I are loving, creative
ideas in the Mind of God. We are already safe at home in this
very moment. Our "tiny, mad idea" of being separate from God is
already finished with. It's like Dorothy in *The Wizard of Oz*, waking up and realizing that she never left home. We simply haven't

accepted that we're already home, and so we continue to hang on to guilt and fear, and we dream that we're separate.

The core source of anxiety is our unconscious guilt and fear, and that's why any strategy to try to solve these problems outside our minds is going to have limited effectiveness. But we can slowly and gently learn to look at our inner sources of anxiety with our Inner Therapist and learn to undo them, waking up to the realization that we're already home. To do this, we have to learn to distinguish between the Voice of our Inner Therapist and the voice of the ego. We'll get started on that next.

Questions for Reflection

1. Have you ever had fears that you knew didn't make any sense, but still you couldn't let go of them? What positive payoffs might they have had?

2. Does eternal bliss sound boring to you? I once overheard some teenagers talking about *Star Wars*. One of them said he'd join the dark side anytime because the light side was boring. Do you ever think that you're hooked on the world's confusion, suffering, and drama?

3. Can you see any connections between the typical problems of the world and your own beliefs and attitudes?

CHAPTER THREE

Two Voices, Two Choices

If you knew Who walks beside you on the way
that you have chosen, fear would be impossible.

A Course in Miracles, T-18.III.3:2

Waking up from the dream of anxiety is a gentle, gradual, and loving process. To move from anxiety to love, we have to learn to distinguish between the two voices in our mind and choose the voice we want to listen to. For each of us, there is a part of our mind that is sane and a part that is insane. The sane part is our Inner Therapist, who is the link back to remembering our Loving Source. The insane part is the ego, which believes itself to be exiled from its Source, and which views the body as its home and ally.

Turn on the nightly news, and you'll instantly see ego insanity in action. The world is full of it. In the twisted theme park that is this earthly realm, dream figures utterly convince us of our separation from one another. This park has two attendants who are present to us during every moment of our visit. One is the ego, and the other is our Inner Therapist. We can hear both their voices, but the "ego always speaks first" and loudest (ACIM T-5.VI.3:5).

By choosing to listen to your Inner Therapist instead of the ego, you can repurpose every experience you go through in this theme park, changing it from an attempt by the ego to keep you asleep into an effort by the Inner Therapist to help you wake up.

The ego might tell you that you need to win tons of shiny tokens in the boardwalk games in order to be happy. Your Inner Therapist will tell you that winning or losing those tokens doesn't define who you are, and your safety doesn't depend on winning. When the roller coaster breaks down and you're stuck in mid-air, the ego will tell you you're vulnerable and should be terrified. Your Inner Therapist will remind you to think of the experience as an opportunity to trust that you are safe no matter what the circumstances. When you eat too much cotton candy and get a bellyache, the ego will use that as evidence that you must be a body. Repurposed through your Inner Therapist, the bellyache becomes an opportunity to learn that you are not your body.

Because the ego belief was made out of our feeling guilty for seemingly separating from our Source, it isn't capable of satisfying us: it is only capable of delivering dissatisfaction. For example, think of the last time you wanted something like a new car, a new job, a new relationship, or a new outfit. Once you finally attained it, did it sustain your happiness? Did the thrill of retail therapy or bingeing on chocolate cake make you permanently joyous? Nope. You may feel short-term happiness, but it doesn't last. Anything the ego tells you that you need ultimately will not satisfy you. The ego is not the voice that wants to make you truly happy.

Yet the ego voice is really compelling. Recently, I had a very *un*peaceful encounter with a friend and former colleague, Teri. Throughout years of working together, we had exchanged many personal stories and developed an affectionate relationship. Yet my file of judgments against Teri included the belief that she tends not to take responsibility for her actions. During a phone call, we were discussing a recent event in the news related to drug use. Teri said something that seemingly contradicted a story she had previously shared with me. With "good intentions," I decided to point out that there was a discrepancy between what she had said then and what she was saying now. Here's how the phone conversation went:

Teri said, "I have never done drugs in my life, and I never would."

"But you told me a year ago that you had tried something with some friends," I responded innocently, but quite sure of myself.

Teri exploded. "How dare you! I never said that!" she yelled in a very loud and adamant voice. "I *never* said that! You are a horribly judgmental person. You should be ashamed of yourself with your 'holier than thou' attitude."

I immediately felt my body tense, my stomach tighten, and agitation flood my veins. *What is happening?* I asked myself.

"You're a liar!" Teri continued angrily. "You're taking something I said and twisting it around! You're so judgmental!"

The ego in my mind rose up to defend myself as the innocent victim of these accusations. Yet I recognized, dimly, that Teri felt she was the victim of *my* words. Where did this leave me? In righteous indignation, of course. In my head, the ego was screaming, "Defend yourself! You were only trying to help Teri look at herself. You are being wrongfully accused!! Fix Teri's perceptions, because *they* are wrong!"

But I knew where defending myself and attacking Teri would lead because I've gone down this road *many* times before. In other words, when I give my allegiance to the ego, I end up with a closed cycle of attack and defense with no way out. My defenses would always justify my position, making me "right" and anyone else "wrong" (for instance, I might say, "Teri, *you're* the one misperceiving because *you* are not remembering correctly"). Whenever this negative cycle is in control, I'm left feeling angry and utterly without peace. I knew I didn't want to attack back, even though I was already feeling the urge in my heart. What to do?

I knew that there was no way of finding true resolution by argument. Any attempt to fix Teri's perceptions would just keep the ego's games going. My job was to be willing to allow the Love in me to join with the Love in Teri, even though the ego in me wanted to clash with the ego in Teri. Teri was asking me, without knowing it, to listen to my Inner Therapist instead of the ego, because there was no other way out of the situation. Despite the ego's firm objections and the habitual desire to attack back, I was willing to give it a try. One of my favorite quotes came to mind: "Do you prefer that you be right or happy?" (ACIM T-29. VII.1:9). I want happy, please.

Still feeling angry and hurt after we hung up the phone, I turned to my Inner Therapist: "I have no idea what to do! I don't want to react from ego and be 'right,' even though the pull to defend myself and attack is strong. I'm really upset. Help!"

In response to this inner plea, only five words came up for me: "I love you" and "I'm sorry." So, in an email, that was all I conveyed to Teri. In this situation, I listened to my Inner Therapist instead of the shrieking ego. And then I considered that perhaps I had "hired" Teri to give me this opportunity to choose for healing.

When I spoke to Teri next, the shift was palpable. It was as if we were both lifted "above the battleground" (ACIM T-23.IV). Teri said that she understood I had not meant to hurt her, and she seemed to let go of her interpretation of the situation, as I had been willing to let go of mine. Teri's perceptions changed not because I proved her wrong, but because I had turned to my Inner Therapist as my guide instead of the tempting ego. Although Teri did not admit that she had experimented with drugs, I sensed that she had a lot of guilt attached to this issue and wasn't ready to go there, hence the explosion. I realized it was not my job to correct Teri from my ego. If I see failings in Teri's ego, it's only because I'm seeing through my own ego (ACIM T-9.III.3:1).

Listening to Your Inner Therapist

You might now be asking, "How do I hear my Inner Therapist? How do I distinguish between the voice of the ego and the Voice of my Inner Therapist?" This takes practice, and we'll explore some ways to do it. I have worked with many people who have felt paralyzed in making decisions because they were unsure whether their "guidance" was coming from ego or from their Inner Therapist. But ultimately, you don't have to worry about figuring it out. As long as you are willing to consistently turn to your Inner Therapist, you can be certain that any ego that is present will gently fall away as you are ready to let it go. The more you do this, the better you will become at distinguishing between these two voices.

In my experience, the voice of the ego is any thought that is judgmental or fearful, or has a negative sense of urgency to it (like "You better do this *now*, or else!"). It makes you feel unworthy, and it limits your sense of self to a body. Because "the ego always speaks first," it grabs most of our time and attention. But the good news is that your Inner Therapist "does not speak first, *but He always answers*" (ACIM T-6.IV.3:2).

The Voice of our Inner Therapist is very quiet — so quiet that it is easily drowned out by the endless distractions of the world. This Voice is a loving and gentle teacher that I experience not as words or sound, but as a feeling — a lightness at the core of my being. Although the body is not our true reality, it can be used as a communication device once we give its purpose over to our Inner Therapist instead of to ego. That means we can actually sense the Voice of the Inner Therapist in our own body.

ACTIVITY:
TUNING IN TO GUIDANCE IN YOUR BODY

I learned this meditation from my friend and teacher, John Mark Stroud, who suggests that the voice of the ego and the guidance of our Inner Therapist communicate through two different channels, like different radio stations. We tune in to the ego's channel all the time, but we are just as capable of tuning in to our Inner Therapist's channel instead. We can practice tuning in to our Inner Therapist's guidance through the following exercise. I highly recommend that you listen to the version in my podcast with John Mark at FromAnxietyToLove.com/Episode8.

Sit quietly and close your eyes. Pay attention to how your body is feeling, then say to your Inner Therapist: "Inner Therapist, please direct my attention to the place in my body where I can most easily attune myself to your guidance." Pause and see where your attention goes. Wherever your attention landed in your body, release that place, and then repeat: "Inner Therapist, please direct my attention to the place in my body where I can most easily attune myself to your guidance." Pause, then repeat the request a third time. Identify the part of your body where your attention goes. Tune in to this place in your body when you want guidance. If you begin to lose that contact, repeat the exercise to see whether your point of focus has shifted. Have fun with this, and be patient. It takes practice to tune in to your Inner Therapist.

I can also perceive the Voice of my Inner Therapist as thoughts, but they are very different from the loud, chatterbox thoughts of the ego. These thoughts often come as inspiration, such as when I ask for help with writing. I ask, I pause, and thoughts come forward.

To strengthen my ability to listen to my Inner Therapist, I use the game of solitaire. When I have to make a decision about a move, my first inclination is to move the card quickly to an obvious spot. However, I've practiced slowing down the process, inwardly asking for assistance in placing my cards. I sit without making a move until I feel an energy that's brighter, quieter, and more spacious than my initial ego feeling of "Move this game along, sister!" Using solitaire as a listening exercise, I am repurposing the goal of the game from winning to slowing down and simply paying attention.

A simple game like solitaire can remind us that in every moment we have the power to choose to listen to one of two voices and make one of two choices. Do we listen to the ego's voice and choose to follow its incessant demand to react or attack? Or do we listen to the Inner Therapist's Voice and choose to follow its quiet plan of healing and miracles? This is a decision that we have countless opportunities to practice in the game of life.

And to counter all the guilt that the ego would like to lead us to, our Inner Therapist has a loving miracle to answer with, a "better way" that we can choose to follow, even if we have only a tiny bit of willingness to listen for it (ACIM T-2.III.3:6). This option is the choice for love and an inner peace that is unshaken by external events. If we follow our Inner Therapist, we are choosing healing. If we follow the ego, we are choosing to be separate, willing ourselves to stay in madness.

(?) **Questions for Reflection**

1. In the activity, where did you sense guidance in your body? What might you learn if you mindfully check in with this part of your body throughout the day?

2. What can you do to remind yourself to pause and ask for guidance when you need it?

3. What will your life look like if you listen to your Inner Therapist instead of the ego?

CHAPTER FOUR

Mental Illness, Mental Health

❦

"But I don't want to go among mad people," Alice remarked.
"Oh, you can't help that," said the Cat:
"We're all mad here. I'm mad. You're mad."
"How do you know I'm mad?" said Alice.
"You must be," said the Cat,
"or you wouldn't have come here."

Lewis Carroll, *Alice's Adventures in Wonderland*

*T*he ego, that popular idea of *who I am*, is actually an insane wish *not* to be as we are in Oneness. We're "all mad here" because we identify ourselves as limited to a body and personality. These are fundamental blocks we have placed in the way of knowing our Loving Source. To keep believing that these fantasies are true, we must live in a dream.

Our mind, in which the memory of Oneness still lives, is very powerful. Yet we are constantly disabling much of its power when we choose to block out Love and listen to the ego. If Love is the Source of our real being, and we're actively blocking it, the result is that "you always attack yourself first" (ACIM T-10.II.4:5).

If you're attacking yourself like this — and you're not even aware of doing so — how can you possibly be at peace? Anxiety, depression, sickness, or other expressions of the inner conflict must arise. "Depression is an inevitable consequence of separation. So are anxiety, worry, a deep sense of helplessness, misery, suffering and intense fear of loss" (ACIM W-pI.41.1:2–3).

Even though these feelings may be "consequences" of the separation, we're not actually separate from Love: we only think we are. The memory of who we truly are is actually quite close. Our awareness of Love's presence, which undoes the ego, must be just beneath the surface of our awareness to be able to make the ego feel so vulnerable and act up so much. This is why we struggle so hard with feelings of anxiety.

As anxiety sufferers, we are aware of the fear that exists just below the surface of our minds. We're very sensitive to the pain and guilt of separation: we just don't realize what it is. Using that awareness, we can learn to recognize our anxiety as a gift with enormous potential for spiritual growth. The fact that we have an easy time recognizing fear is a tremendous asset in working with our Inner Therapist. We know when we're not at peace, even if it is a very subtle disturbance. So it follows that if we know we're not at peace, we must have "decided wrongly" (ACIM T-5. VII.6:3).

Feeling Derealized or Depersonalized?

When earthly therapists assess patients for an anxiety disorder, they look for two symptoms of anxiety called *derealization* and *depersonalization*: the feeling of unreality, and the feeling that you are not your body. Mental health providers consider these feelings abnormal, and in fact they can impair our ability to function. But maybe there is a different way to look at them — not as signs that something is wrong with us, but as pointers toward seeing things correctly. This world *isn't* our reality, and we are *not* our bodies.

If you have experienced these feelings related to anxiety, ask yourself, Do these feelings scare me? If they do, it's a sign that the ego is freaking out because you are perceiving its unreality. It doesn't like that! It wants you to stay identified with your self-concept, because that is the ego's chosen rabbit hole. Nothing makes any sense down there, but it's home for most of us regardless.

We're not ready to embrace the idea that this whole world is only a dream, and that's why we wake up every day thinking we are in a body. And that's fine! We must be gentle with ourselves and allow ourselves to be exactly where we are. If we fall into frustration and think we need to be farther along the pathway than we are, we're simply adding fuel to the ego's flame. Instead, we need to treat ourselves with kindness and self-acceptance in order to progress. When you feel fear or frustration of any kind, including any symptoms of anxiety, the best strategy is to take this feeling to your Inner Therapist and ask for a different way of seeing what makes you fearful. Part of the reason for your fear or frustration may well be that you are something much greater than you know.

Turning to our Inner Therapist doesn't mean that anxiety will disappear instantly and disappear forever. What it means is that we now have tools to deal with it — tools that *work*. As we use these tools, over and over, the barriers we've built against Love slowly fall away, and we experience lasting inner peace. This is how we find the way out of our collective mental illness of separation and insanity.

Wrong- and Right-Mindedness

A Course in Miracles uses two key terms to discuss how we work our way out of insanity: *wrong-mindedness* and *right-mindedness* (ACIM C-1.6:1 and C-1.5:2). To understand these terms, let's re-visit the idea that part of the Child Mind is sleeping. This part of our mind has descended deep into fear and is identified as separate self-concepts (i.e., "you" and "me") but still retains the ability to listen to one of two voices: the Inner Therapist or the ego.

When we listen to the ego and choose it as our guide, we are in "wrong-mindedness." This is the recipe for insanity. When we are wrong-minded, we're anxiety stricken, depressed, angry, and often spiteful. We're also in wrong-mindedness when we think we are alone in the world, and that we are fundamentally separate from others. In short, we're wrong-minded when we think we're who we're used to being.

For starters, complete the next sentence with your name:

"I am in wrong-mindedness when I think I am [*your name here*]."

When we learn how to listen to our Inner Therapist, we enter into "right-mindedness." This is the recipe for mental health. We recognize that we know nothing and have been fundamentally mistaken about important things. For instance, we are willing to consider that maybe the body and the material world don't constitute reality. We are willing to be guided, turning over our perceptions to our Inner Therapist so that we may see the truth.

Again, complete the next sentence with your name: "I am in right-mindedness when I realize that I am *not* [*your name here*]." That is, you are something much greater than your mortal, fallible, and limited sense of self. You are also open to right-mindedness when you are willing to consider that there might be another way of looking at a situation, a relationship, or a person.

Mental health is the experience of lasting inner peace. Learning to live in right-mindedness is the equivalent of finding true inner peace in this world. That true peace does not come from anywhere or anything outside us. And learning to live in right-mindedness is exactly what our Inner Therapist is for.

Where Does Anxiety Come From?

When you are anxious, realize that anxiety comes from
the capriciousness of the ego, and *know this need not be.*
You can be as vigilant against the ego's dictates as for them.

ACIM T-4.IV.4:1–2

I used to have trouble identifying with this Course quote because
my personality is anything but capricious. I'm highly dependable
and fairly predictable. I can make decisions and stick to them, and
I don't have trouble making commitments.

But the ego's capriciousness goes deeper, because it is built on
a lie. Think about how easy it is to get knocked off center when
something "bad" happens. The ego's whole world can be turned
upside down in an instant. That's because the ego is simply a belief that *nothing* is actually *something*. There is nothing to trust in,
because there is nothing there.

Think about a time when you were feeling happy and peaceful. Then you took your car in for an oil change, and your me-
chanic discovered it needed a thousand dollars' worth of critical
repairs. Your sense of financial safety was threatened, and your
happiness flew out the window. Or suppose you see an online
news headline warning about a new antibiotic-resistant superbug,
and suddenly you have new fuel for your fears. This is the capricious ego at work, easily knocked off balance by the threats it
perceives — and it is always on the lookout for them because that
is its way of "protecting" us.

Trying to find stability in life by identifying with the ego is
like trying to stand in balance on a swaying fun-house floor. We
might find our balance with practice, but it's still really easy to get
knocked over. All it takes is an unexpected event or a new threat
to our specialness, and our whole world gets turned upside down.

Anxiety comes from our identification with the ego. The ego uses anxiety as a grand distraction to keep us from remembering our Oneness. It scrambles to muster all the diversions it can, including anxiety, depression, conflict, or sickness. It will tell you that you are all alone. It will do anything to prove that you are limited to a very vulnerable body. But as we remember that our identity is not based in a body, anxiety *has* to fall away.

The more I identify with the body, the more I think I am alone in this world; and the more I cling to this world, the more anxiety I feel. If you want to know just how identified with the ego you are, check your anxiety level. It's a great barometer of your inner storms.

ACTIVITY:
READING YOUR ANXIETY BAROMETER

Anxiety increases when we identify with the small-s self (ego). Anxiety decreases as we develop a stronger identification with our capital-S Self (Spirit).

Draw a scale from −10 to +10, with a zero in the middle. This is your anxiety barometer. The side with negative numbers indicates anxiety levels, with −10 being paralyzing anxiety and −1 being mild anxiety. Zero is neutral. The side with the positive numbers indicates your level of inner peace, with +1 being mild inner peace (feeling relatively calm, but still vulnerable to getting upset) and +10 being an unshakable inner peace (the feeling that regardless of external circumstances, you are at peace because you fully know that nothing can change our eternal reality).

1. In general, where would you rank yourself on the barometer today? Choose a number. Your number may be based either on your mental state or on sensing your body and noticing how much tension or calmness is present.

2. Now let's redefine the scale. Minus 10 indicates a very strong identification with your small-s self. Plus 10 indicates a very strong identification with your capital-S Self.

What does this number tell you about who you think you are? Chances are you recognize that you are somehow identified with being a small-s self. In other words, you strongly identify with being [*your name here*]. With no judgment and no guilt for identifying with the small-s self, use this affirmation to remind yourself of what is in store as you come to embrace your capital-S Self:

There is a part of me that is whole, safe, and at complete peace. This part of me is my Self. As I come to know this Self, my anxiety has to fade. I do not judge myself for where I am. I do not feel guilty for identifying with my small-s self. But I am willing to learn that my happiness and my peace lie in my Self. Inner Therapist, show me the way.

And now rest in trust that the way will become clear. Feel free to repeat this exercise by drawing different scales for different situations, like work, uncomfortable social situations, time with family, or traveling. Whatever the context may be, you can learn how to claim your peace as your Self.

Your Self does not know anxiety. Anxiety comes from trying to be something that we're not. We're not bodies, but we *want* to be bodies. This part of us that actively wants to be separate from Oneness contributes to anxiety. As we learn that Oneness isn't scary and is actually what makes us happy, we gradually open to it, and then anxiety diminishes.

The root cause of anxiety is the sleeping part of our Child Mind, which is dreaming of death and separation. Remember, when we chose to turn away from our Source, this part of our Child Mind felt massive guilt for doing so. It is this part of our mind that causes us anxiety, because it is terrified by the prospect that it actually achieved the separation through listening to the ego and will be punished for it. It's also full of guilt and deep confusion, because it is afraid of God's Love. That Love would be the end of the separation that it's so guilty about, and it's afraid of that, too!

Through our Inner Therapist work, this sleeping part of our Child Mind learns, one miracle at a time, that there is nothing to fear and no reason for guilt. Our Inner Therapist is teaching this frightened part of our mind that it is safe and loved — and that it is in fact part of Love itself. God is not angry, retaliatory, or vengeful. Finally, our reality of eternal love hasn't been changed at all by the part of our Child Mind that is taking a snooze, however dreadful its dreams may sometimes be.

Inner peace returns as we let go of our identity as a body and begin to open the communication channel with Love that we have blocked. We truly want peace. No alien will has ever been thrust upon us, even though we may believe that the "Will of God" is something different from our own will. We're simply learning to remember that we share the Will of God, which is to know who we truly are. God's Will and our will are identical, and God's Will for us is "perfect happiness" (ACIM W-pI.101). This happiness comes through true healing, which we'll learn about next.

Healing versus Fixing

There is a difference between making a symptom go away and healing the root cause of the problem. In my work as a therapist and coach, I often notice that people want their painful struggle to cease, but they also want to keep on doing what they've been doing that causes the pain. A good example is a person who receives a diagnosis of diabetes and begins to take insulin but continues to eat lots of sugary, refined food and doesn't increase her level of exercise.

The same holds true for our identity. We want the pain of our lonely self to go away, but we also want to hold on to our habits of thinking, feeling, and perception: that is, we resist any challenges to our ego or our beliefs about the nature of reality. In other words, we're saying: "I want to be separate and stay in the dream, but I want it to be painless and have everything turn out the way I want." We are declaring that we want to fix the predicament we've gotten ourselves into without healing the state of mind that led us here.

The same is true of anxiety, which can be either *fixed* or *healed*. When anxiety is merely fixed, it is like a leaky pipe. We plug up one hole through positive thinking or some other intervention, only to spring another leak elsewhere. Maybe you've worked hard to get over a phobia of flying, but you still feel panicky about germs. Fixing anxiety means that it is free to return in some other form, because the source of the pain (the belief in separation) has not been healed. Fear is a shape-shifter, and until we heal the belief in separation that gives rise to all fear, that fear will be free to manifest itself as sickness, lack, loneliness, or conflict.

Fixing is what most of us want, even if we usually call it healing. All we want is for the symptoms to go away: we don't want to change anything beyond that. We want the pain to diminish, but we want to keep our world "real," exactly as it is. We want to remain special and separate, but without any difficulties.

When anxiety is *healed*, however, it is effectively eliminated at its source. Healing anxiety begins with not being afraid to look deeply into our minds to see where the anxiety is coming from. In true healing, the anxiety goes away because we experience a fundamental shift in understanding who we really are. Once that's achieved, anxiety no longer serves the purpose of keeping us identified with our body and believing that we have pulled off the separation. There is no unconscious guilt or fear for the anxiety to grab on to, and nothing else arises to take its place. Healing is a gradual process, however, so we can view any recurrences of anxiety as opportunities to work with our Inner Therapist.

Once, after some intensive work with my Inner Therapist, I felt a surge of anxiety. Instantly, an image came to mind of a dark, screeching mass of fear arising out of a black hole, flailing its arms. But the walls of the hole were clean and smooth, and with nothing to grab on to, the anxiety fell back down the hole and disappeared. What this image meant was that there was no belief, thought, or feeling within me for the anxiety to take hold of.

It is really important to get clear on whether you want your anxiety fixed or healed. Be really honest about this. There is nothing wrong with just wanting to fix anxiety because you're not ready to make bigger changes, but you must acknowledge where you are, and look at your current situation with the Inner Therapist. Eventually, you'll recognize that what you really want is healing.

And healing is not possible unless and until we turn to our Inner Therapist. That begins the process of teaching the Child Mind that there is nothing to fear. The next section of the book takes you through the lessons and insights that helped me in overcoming anxiety. It is up to you to put these principles into action.

PART TWO

❧❧

The Ascent
into
Peace

CHAPTER FIVE

Onions, Fear, and the Recipe for Healing

❦

*I*f you've watched the movie *Shrek* as many times as I have, you'll remember the scene where Shrek and the Donkey talk about how ogres are complex and layered, just like onions. Like ogres and onions, people have layers, too. But rather than layers to our personalities, the layers I'm referring to are layers of fear.

When I was young, my sister and I used to take the cushions off our couch and make sandwiches out of each other. One cushion went on the floor, then one of us would lie on top of it, and the other would pile on more cushions. We'd add as many cushions and pillows as we could until we couldn't see what was underneath, and all we could hear was a muffled voice.

Our descent into fear and anxiety works the same way. When our Child Mind had a temper tantrum in its desire for specialness and descended into fear, each step we took into fear was another cushion that muffled our awareness of Love. Each one of these cushions represents a layer of fear, including conscious fears (like fear of what others think) and unconscious fears (like the fear of God). It is these layers of self that prevent us from knowing the peace of who we really are.

Underneath all those layers, Love is always there, even if all we occasionally recognize is a faint echo of something that we've hidden. We may hear that echo in our waking state when we are inspired by music or feel overwhelming love looking into a child's eyes. Yet it is still just an echo of something greater — something we've forgotten and used to hold very dear.

We are still covering Love with more muffling layers of self *right now*. We do it every time we let the ego be our guide (siding with wrong-mindedness), rather than our Inner Therapist (siding with right-mindedness). Our sleeping Child Mind keeps burying our awareness of Love's presence in cushions because it *wants* to stay separate while still feeling guilty about it. The unconscious guilt and fear we carry runs deep, but our Inner Therapist will help us heal.

How the Inner Therapist Heals

The Inner Therapist's job is to help us heal our minds of the layers of fear that muffle the presence of Love. As Love is restored to our awareness, the perception of separation dissipates, and we experience unshakable inner peace. Our Inner Therapist helps us go from anxiety to Love by separating the false from the true, so that only Love remains. But what does this really mean?

Our Inner Therapist has two jobs. One is to be in perfect communication with God; the other is to perceive what is of value in the dreams we are dreaming, which is Love. Whatever we feel and whatever we struggle with, our Inner Therapist has not forgotten that we are part of Love. It is our Inner Therapist's task to undo the mess of mistakes we have made, looking straight through our dreams to the truth beyond them.

However, our Inner Therapist can undo our mistakes and nightmares only if we don't hide them. To let it do its job, we have to be willing to hand things over. To understand the Inner Therapist's function, think of the 1971 film *Willy Wonka and the Chocolate Factory*. Remember the golden geese? Those beautiful geese laid giant golden eggs that dropped down onto a scale beneath the nest, where they were judged to be either good or bad. A good egg was polished and shipped into the world. A bad egg went down the trash chute.

We're like those golden geese, laying eggs all the time. Eggs represent our thoughts, feelings, situations, and experiences, which are all coming *from* us. Remember that "projection makes perception": everything that seems to happen *to* us is actually coming from our sleeping yet hyperactive mind. We are the dreamer of this dream: "The secret of salvation is but this: that you are doing this unto yourself" (ACIM T-27.VIII.10:1).

Our Inner Therapist is our scale. All the "eggs" that we lay get labeled as either true or false, as love or fear. Something that is true lasts forever, a loving gift for all of creation. If something is false, our Inner Therapist actually doesn't toss it down the trash chute, because it doesn't destroy anything that we've made. God honors even our miscreations. Our Inner Therapist simply looks past what is false to the truth beyond it.

For instance, let's say I'm having jealous thoughts and emotions about someone I love. The Inner Therapist does not share my feelings of jealousy, but it does share the feelings of love. So the love is reinforced, and the jealousy is not. When I turn to my Inner Therapist in this situation, my jealousy can fall away. The Inner Therapist overlooks the false emotion and reinforces only the truth, thereby cleaning up that bad egg to keep only the truth and love that it contains. So nothing and no one goes down the chute. What is false is simply not real: it is part of the dream.

But we get into trouble because we love all our shiny golden eggs. We made them, and we love them so much we really don't want to give them to the Inner Therapist to weigh on that scale. We decide that we're going to sort out the good eggs from the bad ourselves. We don't need our Inner Therapist.

When the ego tries to do the Inner Therapist's job, it is problematic because the ego is not a good judge: it doesn't truly know how to choose Love. It wants to remain in charge of solving all the problems it creates. We need the Inner Therapist to help us because it is outside the ego's closed thought system (though very much within our whole mind). So be on the lookout for any temptation that arises to try to solve problems without the help of your Inner Therapist.

Here's a simple example. I recently had a day where I felt bogged down by all the tasks on my plate. I had a video blog to post, papers to grade, an important speaking engagement to prepare for, and laundry to do. I was also scheduled to be a guest on a podcast. By now, I know that I can bring my feelings and my tasks to my Inner Therapist and ask for help. When I genuinely do this, I often experience a sense of ease and flow. On this particular day, however, I wanted to do it all myself. I enjoyed the feeling of accomplishing something "by myself," despite being miserable and stressed out. As I crossed each item off my to-do list, instead of relief, I felt only more pressure to get the next thing done. Only after I was exhausted and depleted did I become willing to "choose again" (ACIM T-31.VIII.3:2). Once I paused and asked my Inner Therapist for help, I felt I was back in the flow, and a sense of ease washed over me. Everything that needed to get done was accomplished without strain.

Offering our feelings, obligations, and judgments to the Inner Therapist for sorting may feel like we're losing something, but there is no loss at all. Instead, it is an exchange. When we give our trouble to the Inner Therapist, we gain a miracle — that is, a shift in perception and a restored awareness of love. We step into right-mindedness. This is the recipe for inner peace.

Unless we give all our golden eggs to our Inner Therapist, the false won't be sorted from the true. Our Inner Therapist is not going to interfere if we want to keep those eggs for ourselves. It will just patiently wait until we're in such a mess that we finally ask for help. The Inner Therapist does not impose its will on us — ever.

As we learn to ascend into the peace we never really lost, we need to allow the Inner Therapist to undo every mistaken thought we made in the descent into fear. This is why we go through challenging times. They are opportunities to truly heal the mind of its layers of fear — not just to temporarily fix or run away from anxiety. "Trials are but lessons that you failed to learn presented once again, so where you made a faulty choice before, you now can make a better one" (ACIM T-31.VIII.3:1).

Maybe there's an issue you've been refusing for years to deal with: a trauma, a betrayal, or something you feel guilty about. Maybe you dealt with something as best you could at the time, but it is coming up again: that stressed-out eating pattern you thought you were over, that family member you thought you had forgiven, or that phobia you thought you had healed. No matter what it is, it is coming up because it is an opportunity to look at another layer of fear with your Inner Therapist and experience healing. To make the most of the healing process, meditation can be an extremely useful tool.

How Meditation Can Help with Healing

Even when we become very diligent at remembering to ask our Inner Therapist for help, if we don't know how to be quiet and listen, we're not going to receive the miracle that is waiting to be recognized. Meditation, whether it lasts one minute or one hour, is a key practice in developing a relationship with your Inner Therapist.

You might be thinking, "I can't meditate. My mind races and is full of chatter." If this is you, there is good news: you *can* meditate. I teach a type of meditation that you can practice even with your eyes open, as you take out the garbage. It is called *mindfulness*. And it helps greatly with what the Course refers to as "mind training" (ACIM T-1.VII.4:1).

Mindfulness meditation is all about accepting the present moment without judgment. That's uncommon, because we're usually lost in reviews of the past or worries about the future. With mindfulness, we can use different perceptions to anchor ourselves to the present moment — like sensing our breathing, sensing the body, becoming aware of sound, or becoming aware of a feeling of love. All these experiences occur only in the present moment, so we can use them to help reorient our mind to the "now." Your Inner Therapist is also in the present moment. So learning how to focus on the here and now, and accepting your present experience without judgment, will help with overcoming anxiety.

There are two ways to practice mindfulness meditation. The formal approach involves sitting down and closing your eyes. The informal approach simply means paying attention to whatever you're doing in the present moment. For instance, when you are brushing your teeth, rather than thinking about everything you have to do today or tomorrow, you focus on the sensation of the toothbrush in your mouth and notice the taste of the toothpaste.

Each time you catch your mind drifting (which will happen often), you simply notice that your awareness has drifted and gently shift it back to brushing.

Just as mindfulness can be practiced formally or informally, you can practice strengthening your relationship with your Inner Therapist. Formal practice means that you sit down, close your eyes, and practice a meditation, such as a guided meditation from this book or a Course workbook lesson. As we build a habit of turning to our Inner Therapist, we learn that we can do so informally, even in busy moments. As we turn to our Inner Therapist more consistently, the entire day becomes a meditation, driven by the continual desire to know the truth of who we are.

Simply remembering to turn to our Inner Therapist requires mindfulness. Becoming aware of unconscious guilt, noticing fearful thoughts that arise in your mind, and acknowledging where you are unwilling to heal all require mindful attention. The meditations in this book are designed to move you from anxiety to love through mindfulness and miracles. Meditation will be very helpful in reinforcing your healing.

A Simple Three-Step Recipe for Healing

Healing is very gentle. Layers of fear surface as you are ready to look at them with your Inner Therapist. The purpose of working through anxiety is always to locate the root of the problem: my mistaken identity with the idea that I am separate, only a body with a brain. I am not Corinne. You are not [*your name here*]. You and I are holy Children of Love who are dreaming and misusing the awesome power of our minds to make the dream seem real.

To clean up the layers of fear we've piled on top of our awareness of Love's presence, there is a specific recipe we can follow for any form of trouble, such as anxiety, a specific situation, or bodily distress.

1. Be willing to see the problem differently.
2. Give your willingness to see the problem differently over to your Inner Therapist and ask for the miracle.
3. Rest in trust that it is done.

This approach is quite simple and very gentle, but we like to make it complicated. We're actually asked to do very little in the process of healing, and the ego finds this insulting! Because we like to make things complicated, I'll expand on this basic recipe in the following chapters.

Chapters 6 and 7 present ten peace-inducing steps, which are things to *do* in our journey from anxiety to love. Chapter 6 introduces steps 1–5, which are focused on handing our perceptions over to our Inner Therapist. Chapter 7 explains steps 6–10, which strengthen this choice.

Chapters 8 and 9 provide ten peace-inducing perception shifts, which are things to *think* that can help us on the path to peace. Though not strictly sequential, these shifts become progressively deeper.

These chapters also contain corresponding mind-straightening mantras. These are either quotes from the Course that helped me or Course-inspired thoughts that were given to me by my Inner Therapist along the way. Use these mantras if you're struggling. Write them down as healing reminders.

You will also find journal prompts to get you writing and reflecting. I am a huge fan of writing in a journal. If someone ever read my journal, they would probably think I was the most miserable person in the world, because I usually only write in it when I'm in pain and working through something. My journal is a tool for finding out what I need to look at with my Inner Therapist. I write until I feel peace again.

I used to go through many journals; now it takes me years to get through one. You'll have to find the pace that works for you. But I encourage you to start writing things out if you feel like you're struggling — even if you don't initially know what you're going to say.

The remainder of the book includes additional meditations designed to help you progress in the journey from anxiety to love. To download three free audio recordings of guided meditations, visit FromAnxietyToLove.com/Meditations.

CHAPTER SIX

Five Steps to Handing It Over

⁂

*T*he ego is insidious. It wants to come along on your spiritual journey and will sneak in without your even realizing it, leaving you with a fake spiritual ego. Although the healing process can really occur in three simple steps — find your willingness to see differently, give your willingness to your Inner Therapist, and trust that it is done — I find that I often need more ways to separate myself from the ego because it hangs on so tightly. Or, perhaps, because *I* hang on to *it* so tightly.

The five steps in this chapter are ways of looking at the ego with our Inner Therapist. We need to look at it in every manner we can, because the ego doesn't *want* to be examined. The ego will always shy away from the light of Love, because if we see it through the eyes of Love, we'll see it for what it really is — nothing!

These steps are inspired by the healing process that the Course teaches. You can use them to work through anxiety, a difficult relationship, or any other problem. They will take you through finding your willingness, recognizing your problems, and handing over what's bothering you to your Inner Therapist.

Let's begin with one of the most fundamental concepts: willingness.

Step 1: Find Your Willingness

We have repeated how little is asked of you
to learn this course. It is the same small willingness
you need to have your whole relationship transformed to joy;
the little gift you offer to the Holy Spirit for which He gives
you everything; the very little on which salvation rests.

ACIM T-21.II.1:1—2

Willingness is the key to happiness. It all starts with just a bit of openness to seeing things differently from how you currently see them. When we are still strongly identified with our ego personalities, we want to make things hard, so we think we have to make enormous efforts in order to change. But cascades of miracles can happen just from a tiny bit of willingness. Your Inner Therapist takes care of the rest. Although we might not at first be ready to receive the gifts that are already ours, they will be there when we are ready for them.

Where is my willingness and how do I find it? The process is simple. Ask yourself, Am I willing to see this differently? If the answer is yes, you've found your willingness.

Often, though, if we are open and honest with ourselves, we might acknowledge that we are *not* willing to let go of a grudge, to see something differently, or to let something go. We are stuck in our way of seeing things and have put up a block to truth and peace. We want it our way, dammit! If we pay attention, we may notice our peace fading away with that obstinate choice.

If I recognize that I really don't want to see something differently (that is, I'd rather be right than happy [ACIM T-29. VII.1:9]), there is a process that helps me find my willingness, however removed from the present it may be. So I ask myself, Am I willing *to be willing* to see this differently?

When you can answer this affirmatively, you've found the tiny bit of willingness that's needed. Touch that tiny bit of willingness, then offer it to the Inner Therapist.

When your fear feels intense, ask yourself whether you are willing to see this situation differently. If so, you have found your willingness.

LET'S MEDITATE: WILLINGNESS

This is a meditation to help you connect to your willingness, which is the birthplace of miracles. Use it whenever you need a shift in perception about a situation in your life.

Begin by taking a few mindful breaths.

Sense *this breath in*, and *this breath out*.

Bring your awareness to something that is currently troubling you: a conflict, a relationship, a feeling of fear.

Ask yourself, "Am I willing to see this differently?" Notice your answer. If the answer is yes, you've found your willingness.

If the answer is no, ask yourself, "Am I willing *to be willing* to see this differently?" If yes, you've found your willingness. If no, repeat the question one or two more times, and be patient with yourself until you find your willingness.

Hold your feeling of willingness in your awareness. Notice if you sense your willingness in a specific place in your body.

Imagine a sense of opening, a clearing, a place for the shift to come in.

Now that you've found that tiny bit of willingness to see differently, imagine turning to your Inner Therapist, your Higher Mind. Offer that willingness to your Inner Therapist and ask for a shift in perception.

Feeling your desire for that shift in perception, for a miracle, say to yourself, "Now let a new perception come to me" (ACIM W-pII.313).

If you notice hesitation or reluctance arising, look at those feelings. Perhaps you have already decided what outcome you want. If so, find your willingness to release the outcome. Then find your willingness to see the reluctance differently as well, and offer that to your Inner Therapist.

Resting in trust that the shift has happened, know that you'll receive the miracle the instant you are ready for it.

✓ **Action Step Recap**

1. When fear arises, check in with your willingness.
2. Ask yourself, "Am I willing to see this differently?" If the answer is yes, you've found your willingness.
3. If the answer is no, ask yourself, "Am I willing *to be willing* to see this differently?" When the answer is yes, there is your willingness!

Mind-Straightening Mantras

- I am willing to see things differently.
- I am willing to be willing.
- "I am determined to see things differently" (ACIM W-pI.21).

Journal Prompts

- What am I willing to look at with my Inner Therapist?
- What am I not willing to look at with my Inner Therapist? Why?
- Where am I attached to an outcome? Am I willing to release the outcome? If not, why not?

Step 2: Commit to an Attitude of Radical Self-Honesty

The opposite of honesty is denial, and denial is a very strong device for ego self-protection. We use denial for concealment all the time, whether or not we realize it. We deny that we are made only of Love, then look to the world to fill the void we feel inside. We get upset because we feel judged by another person; if we were honest, we'd have to admit that we judged them first, and hey, we'd rather deny that. We have frequent thoughts of fear, but we deny that they are there by quickly distracting ourselves.

Take, for instance, that momentary flash of satisfaction that you may feel when you learn you are better off than someone you regard as a rival. Although this may be hard to admit, if you look closely, chances are you will notice an occasional, tiny ego thought along these lines. Feeling satisfaction at someone else's struggle is not a socially acceptable feeling, so we quickly deny it. Yet denying it is not going to get rid of it. This judgment or "scrap of fear" needs to be looked at and undone.

> You retain thousands of little scraps of fear that prevent the Holy One from entering. Light cannot penetrate through the walls you make to block it, and it is forever unwilling to destroy what you have made.... Watch your mind for the scraps of fear, or you will be unable to ask me to do so. (ACIM T-4.III.7:2–5)

If we don't honestly acknowledge the dark spots in our own minds, they're not going to be transformed and healed.

> Do not leave any spot of pain hidden from His light, and search your minds carefully for any thoughts which you may fear to uncover. (ACIM T-13.III.7:5)

We need to be completely and impeccably honest with ourselves and with our Inner Therapist if we're serious about finding peace that lasts. This means being totally honest about the ugly, socially unacceptable thoughts that zip through our minds, even if they last only a split second. The goal is not to stop having negative thoughts. It's to have none that we would keep from sharing with our Inner Therapist (ACIM T-15.IV.9:2). You do not need to clean up your thoughts before sharing them. Instead, you are being asked to bring them, down and dirty, to the light of your Inner Therapist to allow it to do its job of exchanging your false perceptions for loving perceptions.

If you are anxious, depressed, or troubled in any way, admit it. If you're feeling judgmental, own it. Don't turn away from these feelings. These are red flags signaling that it's time to work — not cues to avoid them, procrastinate, or distract yourself. The most important indicator of how you are doing is how you feel. If you feel anything but pure joy, the ego is at the wheel, driving your car.

✔ Action Step Recap

1. On a scale from 0 to 10 (with 10 being 100 percent honest and transparent), rate your level of honesty with your Inner Therapist. It might take extreme honesty to not automatically give yourself a 10.

2. Ask yourself if you're willing to be more honest with your Inner Therapist.

3. If the answer is yes, make an internal commitment of honesty. Be willing to hide nothing from your Inner Therapist.

4. If the answer is no, you are already being honest with your answer! Remind yourself that freedom from anxiety lies in radical honesty with yourself and your Inner Therapist. Compassionately allow yourself to be where you are, and revisit this step when you are ready.

Mind-Straightening Mantras

- I am willing to be honest with myself and my Inner Therapist, even if I don't like what I see.
- It is okay that I have negative thoughts in my mind. I don't have to deny that they are there.
- Honesty undoes anxiety.

Journal Prompts

- What prevents me from being 100 percent honest with my Inner Therapist?

- What am I afraid will happen if I am 100 percent honest with my Inner Therapist?

Step 3: Look Directly at What Is Coming Up for You

Once you are committed to an attitude of honesty, you are ready to look directly at what is coming up inside your mind.

You can do this by asking yourself two questions:

1. What am I feeling right now?
2. What thoughts are going through my mind?

The emotions may be intense or subtle, the thoughts may be obvious or fleeting. Either way, we have to examine our minds carefully for the beliefs that block peace. To do this, it's always been helpful for me to make laundry lists of my fears and irritations. Here is a list of my typical fears from my journal:

- I'm afraid I'm going to die.
- I'm afraid of suffering.
- I'm afraid of being sick.
- I'm concerned that situation X is going to turn out a certain way.
- I'm afraid of my loved ones' suffering.
- I'm afraid of letting someone down.
- I'm afraid of losing a relationship.
- I'm afraid of being afraid.

Take a moment to make a laundry list of your own fears. Every fear has a useful purpose when we are committed to a path of healing. Anxieties provide wonderful opportunities to look at our deeply held, ego-driven beliefs. The only way to move through and beyond them is to acknowledge their existence.

But listing our fears is only the first step. We can look at the underlying beliefs that are fueling our fears. Look at each item in your list of fears and ask yourself, "What does this fear show that

I believe?" Make a laundry list of those beliefs. Here is a sample of mine:

- I believe that I am limited to a body.
- I really *do* believe that I am Corinne.
- I believe that I can be hurt and that I can suffer.
- I really do believe in death.
- I believe that I really managed to separate myself from Love.
- I believe more in the world than in God.
- I believe that everything outside of me has to be okay for me to be okay.
- I believe that my body can hurt me.
- I believe that I may be alone.
- I still believe there are some things that can't be forgiven.

Get really honest with yourself about the icky beliefs that you hold. You may feel a strong tendency to turn away from them. The ego does not like being directly examined by you and your Inner Therapist, to work toward its undoing. It might try kicking up more anxiety or fear to prevent you from looking at it, or come up with twenty ultra-important things (like checking Facebook) that absolutely must get done first.

These are ego flare-ups, and having them means you are doing good work! If you experience these tendencies, go at your own pace. Back off if you need to, or ask your Inner Therapist for help. The ego is actually more afraid of Love than it is of fear, and that is why it will resist the counsel of the Voice for Love within you. As the Course tells us, "You have used the world to cover your love, and the deeper you go into the blackness of the ego's foundation, the closer you come to the Love that is hidden there. *And it is this that frightens you*" (ACIM T-13.III.4:4–5).

Don't shy away from anything. Turn toward the pain and

discomfort when you feel ready to, and imagine your Inner Therapist right beside you. You can say to yourself, "I am willing to look at this with my Inner Therapist." It will be comforting to remember that you are not looking at it alone.

For additional practice in noticing fear, experiment with the following meditation.

LET'S MEDITATE: NOTICING FEAR

Anxiety sufferers have a gift: we have a very easy time recognizing even the faintest sense of fear. This meditation is designed to help you turn toward any subtle fear and bring it to the light of Love to be healed.

Ground with the breath: notice it coming in and going out. You can always come back to the breath if you need to orient yourself to the present moment.

Notice any subtle fear in your body or mind. Holding the fear in your awareness, turn toward your Inner Therapist and say, "Inner Therapist, I am willing to look at this fear with you in order to allow it to be undone. I do not want to keep it hidden. I want to know the peace that I am."

Every time we catch a fleeting sense of fear and bring it to the light of Love, we are working to undo every false perception in our mind and to remember who we truly are.

Every time we bring a fear to our Inner Therapist, we benefit, even though we might not immediately recognize how.

Imagine that the fear coming up is a layer of an

onion. As you look at the fear with your Inner Therapist, imagine that the layer is being peeled back and removed. Continue bringing every subtle fear to your Inner Therapist as you notice it. Repeat this process until you have brought every fear that you are aware of to the light of Love for healing, peeling back all the layers of the onion.

Hidden in the center of this onion is your awareness of the Love and peace that you are. You are simply allowing the removal of all blocks to your awareness of this peace.

Rest in trust that peace is already here, and you can accept that peace *now*.

✅ Action Step Recap

1. Ask yourself, "What am I feeling? What thoughts are going through my mind?"
2. Get radically honest. Write down every fear you can think of.
3. Look at each fear and ask yourself, "What does this fear show me that I believe?" Make a list of the underlying beliefs behind each fearful or judgmental thought.
4. Save this list. You'll use it in step 5.

Mind-Straightening Mantra

I noticed that this fearful thought about X just zipped through my mind. I'm willing to look at it with you, Inner Therapist.

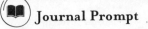 **Journal Prompt**

What does it feel like to write out your fears? What does it feel like to write out the underlying beliefs behind the fears? Does it feel overwhelming, or does it feel like a relief? Whatever your reaction, be honest about it. You are looking directly at what is coming up for you, and this is a courageous thing to do.

Step 4: Acknowledge That the Fear Is Coming from Your Split Mind

What we see "out there" in the world is a reflection, a projection, of what is in our mind.

On a superficial level, this means that if I see Susie as immature, judgmental, and catty, then we can say I must have those qualities within myself. What I don't like in another person is what I don't like in myself, and I'm capable of behaving in exactly the same ways.

The Course, however, goes deeper than this: "I am responsible for what I see. I choose the feelings I experience, and I decide upon the goal I would achieve. And everything that seems to happen to me I ask for, and receive as I have asked" (ACIM T-21. II.2:3–5). Every fear and anxiety that we think of as happening to us originates in the sleeping part of our Child Mind, which believes in an ego. Since part of our Child Mind is asleep, and part of it is awake and home in Love, we can say that it is split. Some of the things that we originate and then project from this place are not so nice. Remember, this sleeping part of the mind holds a lot of guilt and fear.

I'm certainly not implying "New Age guilt," the idea that everything bad that happens is the result of negative thinking, negative attitude, bad karma, or a burden from a past life. The problem actually goes deeper than that. Bad experiences represent the ego's best efforts to keep you believing in the world it has created.

Remember, the goal of the ego is to keep guilt in place. The ego wants to stay separate from our Source, and it can only do so by maintaining our belief in the separation. The ego uses every painful circumstance we find ourselves in to reinforce its message that what we see is real and that we are bodies. Stub your toe, and it hurts. Freak out with a panic attack, and the body goes on full alert! If we follow the ego, we become willing participants in its endless and painful roller-coaster ride.

In the separation theme park, another of the ego's entertaining sideshows is the idea that you are somehow a victim of God's mysterious ways. For instance, how many times have you heard seemingly wise proverbs like these?

> God gives you only what you can handle.
> If God brings you to it, God brings you through it.
> God comforts the disturbed and disturbs the comfortable.

All these ideas place God in the role of comforting you during disturbing life experiences, which is nice. But comforting you after deliberately disturbing you would be cruel and manipulative, and God does not manipulate. God only loves, or, as the Course puts it, "God is but love, and therefore so am I" (ACIM W-pI.171). It is worth repeating that *God does not bring you pain in any form, ever*. God is not separate from you, and all pain and fear is the result of a split mind.

Clearly, we want to find a way to stop calling forth the pain that comes from the belief in ego. Our Inner Therapist has a "better way" (ACIM T-2.III.3:6). All we need is willingness. The Inner Therapist takes everything we've made in this dream and turns it to the service of truth.

Let's recap the steps thus far:

1. You find your willingness.
2. You commit to getting radically honest with your-self.
3. You look directly at what is coming up in you.
4. You acknowledge that the fear is somehow coming from the split mind by saying something like, "God isn't doing this to me; this is just the ego trying to keep me focused on it."

Everything that seemingly happens to you can be an opportunity to wake up, as each situation is repurposed by your Inner Therapist to provide you with a miracle instead of a grievance.

Even if we are feeling anxious and believe that we're helplessly stuck in ego, there is still a quiet, unchanged part of our mind that remains purely at peace. It is possible to be aware of this quiet, still part of our mind even in the midst of turmoil. This awareness is touching the split mind.

The mind is split at two different levels:

1. The unconscious level: Here there is a split between your awake Child Mind, which is still at peace in God, and your sleeping Child Mind, which is anxiously dreaming this wild dream.
2. The conscious level: Here there is a split between the fearful voice of the ego mind (wrong-mindedness) and the loving Voice of our Inner Therapist (right-mindedness).

As we choose to listen to our Inner Therapist instead of ego and experience miracles on the conscious level, the sleeping Child Mind is reminded that there is nothing to fear, and it can reawaken to its truth.

So instead of placing blame on people, situations, or God for causing us anxiety, we can experiment with acknowledging that all fear is coming from the split mind. As we see and learn to heal this split, anxiety falls away. We have the power to see witnesses to fear or witnesses to love. The choice is ours because nothing is outside ourselves.

How Blood Tests Revealed My Split Mind

A while ago, driven by hypochondria, I had to get some extensive blood work. (My apologies to anyone with needle anxiety who is already cringing.) I was very nervous about it but followed through with the appointment anyway.

In the waiting room of the hematologist's office, I was well aware that the people around me were not well. Many of them were there for chemotherapy; that thought alone made me extremely uncomfortable, and I wanted to bolt out the door. But I didn't.

As the nurses prepped my arm to take blood, I explained why I was there. Each time I named a symptom I had, one particular nurse would respond, "That's not good." Then, while drawing blood, she said, "You had better not pass out on me!" So guess what I did. I had a surge of anxiety resulting in the typical vasovagal faint response; I turned clammy and pale and nearly fainted. The staff rushed to put my feet up and lay me down, and they brought me gummy worms and juice to raise my blood sugar as the episode passed. When I saw the doctor afterward, he ordered even more extensive lab work, to be completed in a hospital. Great! I hated needles, but I hated hospitals even more.

I could easily go on a rant about the nurse whose insensitive behavior caused me to almost pass out. I did have angry, judgmental thoughts, and I wanted to set her straight. But I remembered the Course principle that sanity lies not in having no angry thoughts, but in *having none that we would keep*. So I felt my angry feelings, but I chose to turn my judgments over to my Inner Therapist so that I might see things differently.

After I left the doctor's office, I was able to look at this situation a bit more objectively. The Course says that we are constantly calling forth witnesses to fear or witnesses to love. That day, I did a superb job of calling forth witnesses to fear. Going in for the tests, I was scared. Everything felt very real, I was completely identified with Corinne, and I was worried that my body could be sick. So I called that nurse forth to reinforce my belief in the situation, and she agreed to this role. This is what happened when I chose to follow the ego as my teacher. (Thanks a lot, ego!)

Then I began laughing (mainly from being exhausted by anxiety), realizing how insane the whole drama had been. I remembered the Course's teaching that I have a split mind on the conscious level (split between the voices of the ego and the Inner Therapist) and unconscious level (split between the sleeping and awake parts of the Child Mind). The Inner Therapist and the awake Child Mind were unaffected by all my fears. I could faintly sense that part of me was still unchanged despite this unpleasant experience, and this awareness was touching the split mind. I could see an icky picture, but I laughed at it, knowing it really had no power over me. I knew deep down that I was safe.

On the following Monday, I went to the hospital for more blood tests. This time, I was determined to call forth witnesses to love. I kept turning to my Inner Therapist, stating my willingness to remember I was not a body and so I was always safe. Despite this willingness, I felt really anxious again. But I was determined to see the situation differently. I embraced the idea that something in me could call forth peace even if the surface of my mind felt anything but peaceful.

I walked into the hospital lab waiting room and recognized the nurse behind the desk as the mother of a friend from college.

"What a relief!" I exclaimed upon seeing a familiar, friendly, loving face. I mentioned that I was a bit anxious, and without my asking, my friend's mom decided to do my blood draw herself. We were able to catch up on recent happenings instead of talking about my symptoms. Although I still felt anxious throughout the experience, I was willing to learn that I am not "Corinne." I got through the procedure without any difficulties or fainting. As I said goodbye, my friend's mom told me something that stopped me in my tracks: She didn't usually work on Mondays. She was called in about thirty minutes before I arrived.

"The miracle does not awaken you, but merely shows you who the dreamer is" (ACIM T-28.II.4:2). Calling forth witnesses for love showed me that I am the dreamer of this dream. It reinforced my trust in my Inner Therapist and in turn reminded the deepest part of my sleeping Child Mind that it has not left God and has nothing to fear. It showed me that there really is no split mind, because we are already home in Love — and that I am a Child of God (like all of us).

You have great power to call forth witnesses to fear at any moment of the day, but you also have the power to call forth witnesses to love. Because of the ego's addiction to fear, you can't call forth witnesses to love by yourself: you must ask the Inner Therapist for help. When you call forth witnesses to fear, however, you are doing so alone. You could say that you're calling forth fear with the ego, but the ego is really nothing: it is just a belief inside our own minds.

To get out of the cycle of calling forth witnesses to fear, you first have to recognize that a fearful situation is coming from your split mind (even if you don't know how). You're not creating it consciously, but no one else is doing it to you — certainly not God. Once you open to the idea that everything that is happening is coming from your sleeping split mind, and that you can therefore call forth witnesses for love or witnesses for fear, then you can immediately give that recognition to the Inner Therapist. Be willing to have experiences that will show you that you are part of Love (God), but refrain from deciding what these experiences should look like. Answers and solutions come in many forms, and not necessarily in ways you expect. A witness for love may simply take the form of a feeling of inner peace. Ask, and you shall receive.

Mind-Straightening Mantras

- I admit that this thought is coming from my split mind, even though I don't know how. I'm willing to look at it with my Inner Therapist.
- "There is no cruelty in God and none in me" (ACIM W-pI.170).
- Nobody is making me think these thoughts. These thoughts are coming from me.
- I am willing to own my projections and then give them to my Inner Therapist so that I can learn to extend Love instead of fear.
- The ego is only a mistaken belief. It has no power to hurt me.
- Although I feel anxiety, I am willing to get to know the peaceful part of my mind, which is available to me now.

Journal Prompt

If everything is coming from the split mind, then nothing outside you can "cause" anything. Resistance to this idea is normal. Explore your own resistance. When are you still tempted to blame outside circumstances or people for your situation? After you have made a list, look at each item and ask yourself, "Am I willing to see this differently?"

Step 5: Give It to Your Inner Therapist and Ask for a Miracle Instead

After looking directly at the perceptions coming up within you and acknowledging that they are coming from your split mind, you can give everything to your Inner Therapist so that it can be transformed.

There are many different ways to express this step:

- Give it to my Inner Therapist.
- Share it with my Inner Therapist.
- Look at it with my Inner Therapist.
- Offer it to my Inner Therapist.

What matters is that you are willing to let go of the way you see things so that your Inner Therapist can do its job: exchanging false perceptions for true perceptions. This shift in perception is a miracle.

I like to think of this step as *looking with* my Inner Therapist at what I have made. To me, the phrase *looking with* requires even less effort than *handing over*. Although this is an internal process, feel free to experiment with writing your concerns or perceptions down on paper and placing the paper in a box or envelope to symbolically represent handing them over to your Inner Therapist.

Try this now:

1. See if you can feel, even for an instant, that you are genuinely placing your concerns in your Inner Therapist's hands.
2. Say emphatically, "Inner Therapist, I give this to you now. Please give me the miracle instead."

The tiniest glimmering of willingness to do this is the same as an all-out hurling of your concerns into your Inner Therapist's hands. Summoning a little willingness is the same as fully letting go.

You can also think about this step as "thought swapping" with your Inner Therapist. You lay out a negative thought, and your Inner Therapist swaps it for a miracle. It's like playing poker and laying your unwanted cards out on the table so the dealer can give you better ones. As you learn that giving your perceptions to your Inner Therapist in exchange for miracles makes you happy, this thought swapping becomes effortless. And it's not magic. Those miraculous thoughts of Love are already in your mind, waiting to be expressed through you.

Although the miracle is already there, however, you might not be ready to receive it. If nothing seems to happen when you give your perceptions to your Inner Therapist, your task is simply to trust that you'll get the miracle when you're ready.

Reminder: we're asked *not* to do the Inner Therapist's job. When something comes up, it is not our task to figure out how to fix ourselves or change our negative thinking. Instead, we can leave correction to our Inner Therapist through our willingness. Our Inner Therapist will choose Love *for* us.

We might find that after we hand something over, we keep picking it back up and worrying about it. We'll look at that in the next chapter.

✓ Action Step Recap

1. Think of a problem that comes up often.
2. Imagine giving that problem to your Inner Therapist, so that you are not keeping it to yourself.
3. Read every item on your laundry list of fears from step 3. As you read each one, pause and say, "Inner Therapist, I am willing to look at this with you. Please give me the miracle instead." Sense that you are not keeping the problem for yourself. You are

sharing it with your Inner Therapist so that it can be transformed.

Mind-Straightening Mantras

- Inner Therapist, I'm willing to look at this with you. (You can "look with" your Inner Therapist by imagining that your Inner Therapist shines its light down on the problem, and the problem dissolves. Similarly, "handing over" your problem is like placing a letter in a mailbox and sending it to your Inner Therapist so you don't have it anymore.)
- Take this thought from me. I want a miracle instead.
- Here you go! I'm placing this in your care, and I'm not picking it back up.
- Here is my tiny bit of willingness, Inner Therapist. You said this is all I need. Now show me the miracle.
- "I am entitled to miracles" (ACIM W-pI.77).

Journal Prompt

How do I think I would do a better job at problem solving than my Inner Therapist? Where does my lack of trust come from? (Ask your Inner Therapist to look *with* you at what you write.)

CHAPTER SEVEN

Five Steps to Strengthening Your Choice

୬ଡ଼ୠ

*I*n the previous chapter, we looked at the first five steps in the "ascent to peace," which covered how to get ready to hand over your troubled thoughts and anxieties to your Inner Therapist — and then to actually do it. As I've said before, this process can be done in three steps or none at all, depending on your commitment to becoming free of fear.

But the ego loves to make things complicated. One of its favorite tactics is to make us forget we ever chose to consult our Inner Therapist — or that one exists at all. To address this typical confusion and forgetfulness, here are five steps to help you remember and strengthen your choice to work with your Inner Therapist.

Step 6: Acknowledge Your Unwillingness to Heal, and Look at That with Your Inner Therapist, Too

The Course emphasizes that we need only a tiny bit of willingness in order for a miracle — a shift in perception — to occur. And this is true! We're asked to do so little. So we hand our situation over to the Inner Therapist, again and again, but we may still feel stuck sometimes. What's going on? Why does it feel like this is all such a struggle?

The answer is that a part of us *wants* some struggle, difficulty, and conflict in order to maintain our belief in a separate self.

We've built blocks against Love because we want to experience ourselves as separate and autonomous. Those blocks keep the ego going. "The ego becomes strong in strife" (ACIM T-5. III.8:8). We're okay with letting a little Love in, but not too much. The call to Love is so strong, however, that the only way to deny it is to be *unwilling* to heal.

Unwilling? Yep. Sigmund Freud called this tendency the "death instinct." We also know it by terms like *self-destructive behavior*, *resistance*, or *self-sabotage*.

The Inner Therapist can't transform something for us if we don't bring it out into the open and hand it over. This requires honesty, openness, and willingness to look at our *unwillingness*. As we do this with our Inner Therapist, we open ourselves up to receiving miracles.

If you feel anything other than a deep sense of peace or experience any degree of struggle, acknowledge it as an unwillingness to heal. Say, "This is where I'm unwilling to heal. Here you go, Inner Therapist!" Keep at it. The universe is "trembling with readiness" (ACIM T-17.II.8:2) to give us all of the gifts that are already there, waiting to be acknowledged.

Experiment with the following meditation for help with bringing unwillingness to your Inner Therapist.

LET'S MEDITATE:
MOVING THROUGH RESISTANCE

This meditation is for anytime you feel stuck in resistance, that is, an *unwillingness* to heal. Part of our mind wants to hang on to fear and guilt, even though they cause pain. The good news is that you can allow resistance to be effortlessly and instantly undone.

Taking three breaths, notice the full duration of each inhalation and exhalation. As you exhale, purse your lips as if you're blowing into a pinwheel to slow down your exhalation.

Bring to mind the resistance you feel, whether it's an active stubbornness or a chronic feeling (such as anxiety) that keeps arising even though you feel you have already given it to your Inner Therapist. Picture the issue or situation and allow yourself to feel being stuck with it.

Say to yourself, "This must be an area where I am unwilling to heal. I need not feel guilty about it. It's okay that this is coming up."

Notice where the feeling of being "stuck" sits in your body. How do you experience this feeling? Is there a heaviness to it? A tightness? Where is it located? In the chest? The belly?

Once you connect with the sensory experience of "stuckness," continue to breathe. Say to your Inner Therapist, "I am willing to look at my unwillingness with you."

Now picture the resistance as an object outside you, and give it a shape and a color. Shrink the resistance down to a size that will fit in your hand. Pick up this small object in your hand. It may feel much heavier than it looks.

Imagine an altar in your mind, which represents the place where the Inner Therapist abides. Repeat, "I am willing to look at my unwillingness with you, Inner Therapist," as you place the small object of resistance on the altar, and add, "Here it is." Imagine that the Love of your Inner Therapist shines forth from the altar, and the object is suddenly transformed into light.

Say to yourself, "I trust that the shift in my perception has been given, and I accept the miracle now."

Continue to breathe, noticing each breath in and each breath out, resting in trust.

Mind-Straightening Mantras

- This persistent fear that won't go away is my unwillingness to heal. There is a part of my mind hanging on to this fearful thought because I still want this world, and I want to stay separate. I'm willing to look at my unwillingness with my Inner Therapist, too.
- Am I willing? If not, am I willing to be willing?
- When I recognize my unwillingness, I can exchange it for a miracle.

Journal Prompt

Make a list of the thoughts or fears that you feel unwilling to share with your Inner Therapist. Look at each item and write down what you fear will happen if you share it. Be honest. For example, you might write, "I am unwilling to give my romantic relationship to my Inner Therapist because I'm afraid it will be taken away from me." Note that this example reflects the belief that God is an "antagonizer" and expects sacrifice. Once you get really clear about your fears, be willing to see them differently. Then revisit each item and say to your Inner Therapist, "In this situation, I am willing to look at my unwillingness with you."

Step 7: Recognize That It Is Done, and There Is Nothing to Fear

This next step is easily overlooked, but essential.

You have genuinely been willing to look at your issue with the Inner Therapist; now comes the time for trust. The Inner Therapist "always answers" (ACIM T-6.IV.3:2). You just may not be ready to hear the answer yet.

The "tiny, mad idea" of separation was healed the instant it emerged. We have not left our Source, and God is not mad at us. We're as safe and unchanged now as we were before the seeming separation began and as we will be when the seeming separation is over. Nothing and no one is out to get us. We cannot die, because we are not these bodies — we only think we are. We are safe. We are healed. We are already home. The "tiny, mad idea" is done, and our nightmares are over. We're simply learning how to remember this.

Now comes the time to steadfastly dig in your heels and refuse to allow your mind to ruminate on the situation. You've handed it over, and it's time to release it. If a disturbing doubt creeps back in, catch it and bring your mind back to this thought: "I've handed this over already — it is done."

In step 5, I suggested writing down your concerns and placing the paper in a box or envelope to represent the act of handing them over to your Inner Therapist. Consider doing this now. Remind yourself that once you place the paper in a box or envelope to hand it over, you cannot worry about it anymore. It is time to accept the miracle and rest in trust.

In practicing this step, I have sometimes realized that I wasn't ready to stop worrying about my problem! I was still attached to controlling the situation and was not ready to fully release it. So if you find that you just can't stay with this idea of resting in trust, then go back to step 6 and acknowledge this as a form of unwillingness to heal. You might have to stay there, or at any of the previous steps, for a while. If you do, don't worry about it. Be exactly where you are, and be kind to yourself.

The ego might also tempt you with thoughts of failure. For instance, you might hand something over to your Inner Therapist, ask for a miracle, and find that nothing happens. You might immediately conclude, "This doesn't work." But if you look closely and with radical honesty, you might see that you have already decided what the outcome should be. Miracles happen all the time. "When they do not occur something has gone wrong" (ACIM T-1.I.6:2). What has likely "gone wrong" is that the ego's voice of doubt has spoken up, or we've developed expectations of what miracles or guidance should look like. If we're plugged in to our own expectations, we're going to miss the gift that is waiting for us. Revisit step 1 and find your willingness to release all expectations in your mind.

Complete trust in our Inner Therapist doesn't happen overnight, and we are not asked to trust it blindly. As we take our perceptions to our Inner Therapist and ask to be shown miracles instead, we have experiences that give the grounds for trust. Remember, you don't have to believe anything I have presented in this book. Just sincerely try working with the principles, and let the results speak for themselves.

Mind-Straightening Mantras

- Inner Therapist, thank you for not leaving us alone.
- Inner Therapist, thank you for what you do!
- I am safe and healed and whole. There is nothing to fear.
- "Let me recognize my problems have been solved" (ACIM W-pI.80).

Step 8: Show Up for Therapy with Your Inner Therapist Daily

A therapist does not heal; *he lets healing be.*

ACIM T-9.V.8:1

During my adult episode of uncontrollable anxiety, I reentered counseling. That helped me look at some psychological issues I needed to address, but then I realized that I had some serious inner work to do with the Course. After several months of therapy, it was time for my Inner Therapist to become my full-time therapist again (though the Inner Therapist can be your full-time therapist even if you are in therapy with a counselor). But I had to show up for my appointments. Showing up for this kind of therapy is more than a daily ritual: it occurs moment to moment. But a daily check-in is a good place to start.

Showing up meant that I needed to spend time reading the Course, writing in my journal, and meditating every day. Previously, I used to do this until I felt better, and then I'd coast...until I found myself in trouble again.

Sit down right now and think about how to commit to your inner therapy. Do you need to schedule time in a planner? What forms of therapy will work for you right now: meditating, reading, writing, or being in receptive silence?

Eventually you're going to turn to your Inner Therapist continually because you want to. You may even realize that you're doing it in your sleeping dreams. I love it when I wake up and realize I was dreaming about handing something to my Inner Therapist, and received a shift in perception in my sleep! This work is about leaving no stone unturned where fear can hide. We get better and better at showing up.

"You can be as vigilant against the ego's dictates as for them" (ACIM T-4.IV.4:2). Showing up for inner therapy is a form of vigilance on behalf of your own happiness. It is a declaration to yourself that *you are worthy of love.*

A key part of showing up is learning how to get quiet and listen. If our minds are constantly full of chatter (which is true for most of us), we're not leaving any room for the miracles the Inner Therapist can bring. Even constantly saying, "I give this to you, Inner Therapist!" can interfere with listening. We must anchor ourselves in the present, for this is where our Inner Therapist abides. "An empty space that is not seen as filled, an unused interval of time not seen as spent and fully occupied, becomes a silent invitation to the truth to enter, and to make itself at home" (ACIM T-27.III.4:1).

Mindfulness meditation has been a huge help for me. It teaches us to be with our present-moment experience exactly as it is (pleasant or unpleasant, noisy or quiet), without trying to change it. The documented health benefits of mindfulness are very impressive. It has been shown to reduce anxiety and depression and boost memory, attention, and the immune system. In the Western world, we're slowly starting to understand that going inward is a positive thing. Try the following mindfulness meditation.

LET'S MEDITATE:
ANCHORING TO THE PRESENT MOMENT

This meditation is for strengthening the mind's ability to focus on the present moment, which is the home of our Inner Therapist. We can use any aspect of our experience to ground ourselves in the present. For this meditation, we're going to use the breath.

Begin by sitting comfortably with both feet on the floor or lying down. Place one hand on your chest and the other hand on your belly. Which hand is moving more: the top hand or the bottom hand?

If your top hand is moving more, your breathing pattern is one that is associated with anxiety and stress. See if you can relax your abdominal muscles and allow the breath to flow in and out from the belly, so that you feel more motion in your bottom hand.

Keep the sensation of the breath in your awareness as the belly expands and contracts. Notice *this breath in,* and *this breath out.*

Each time your mind wanders, simply notice that it wandered and gently return your awareness to the sensation of the breath.

Breath is always in the present moment, so it becomes a beautiful anchor to the here and now. Continue this practice for five minutes. See if you can build up to twenty minutes.

Mind-Straightening Mantras

- I am learning how to be a better listener.
- I want to show up for inner therapy.

- My inner work is key to my happiness.
- "Let me be still and listen to the truth" (ACIM W-pI.106).
- "I will be still an instant and go home" (ACIM W-pI.182).

📖 Journal Prompts

- What do I not want to look at? Am I holding on to a grudge?
- Where does the "busyness" of the ego hook me? What do I prioritize ahead of God?

Step 9: Recognize Unconscious Fear and Guilt as They Arise

The unconscious fear and guilt in our minds comes from our belief that we have turned our back on Love. We also learned that "ideas leave not their source" (ACIM T-26.VII.4:7). Even though our sleeping Child Mind projected this fear and guilt outward, like a baby with projectile vomiting, it is still in our mind. The way to heal it is to look at it with our Inner Therapist. By definition, however, we're not conscious of what is *un*conscious. So our first step in healing unconscious fear and guilt is to become aware that it exists in our minds. We can do this in one of two ways.

Becoming Aware of Unconscious Fear and Guilt

The first approach is to simply work through the steps described above, bringing unwillingness and anxiety to our Inner Therapist. As we do so, unconscious fears surface when we are ready to look at them. Remember, we're like onions: we've got layers upon layers of fear and guilt. We use those layers to keep our awareness of Love (at the center of the onion) hidden. Every time we become willing to look at an aspect of our life with our Inner

Therapist, we are peeling back a layer of the onion. As we continue this process with radical self-honesty, we allow even deeper layers of unconscious fear and guilt to rise to the surface.

This has happened to me a number of times. Most recently, I was quite surprised by the form in which my unconscious fear and guilt showed up. Because I have had some major issues with bodily health, as well as an intense fear of something being wrong with my body, it should be no surprise that the thought of pregnancy and labor has always freaked me out (even in kindergarten). Child rearing also terrified me, because I saw myself obsessing over the health of another body besides my own.

I could have avoided these issues by simply deciding not to have children. However, because my husband made it clear that he wanted children, both of us were forced to look at all our beliefs about children and parenting.

By being willing to look at this issue with my Inner Therapist, I recognized that I believed *it is bad to be here in this world*. In my mind, having kids was equivalent to maintaining the separation, and I feared I would be punished for it. I started to notice that I felt very guilty just for being in this world. This was surprising; I had no idea that I held this belief. It was only through my willingness to keep bringing fears to my Inner Therapist that this idea came to the surface to be looked at and healed. The Course suggests that we all feel guilty because we believe that we pulled off the separation. But we didn't, and we're not guilty. What a relief!

In another case, I noticed a physical symptom in my body that I didn't like. I also noticed that as I focused on the fear of this symptom over a few days, the symptom seemed to grow, and so did the fear. Focusing on the fear made fear grow. I saw how easily I could tumble down the slippery slope of fear if I chose to go down that path.

When I realized that I was actively descending into fear, I was guided to sit down and get quiet. Within a minute, I was prompted to open my Course book at random. Here is the exact sentence that caught my eye: "The body will remain guilt's messenger, and will act as it directs as long as you believe that guilt is real" (ACIM T-18.IX.5:1).

This statement affected me as it never had before, even though I had read it many times in the past. As long as I believe in guilt in *any* form, the body is going to reflect that belief and serve as guilt's messenger. Immediately, I was given the thought, "There is no guilt in me." I said this cleansing phrase to myself many times over, and I encourage you to say it to yourself as well.

Then I realized something else: *If there is no guilt in me, that also means there is no guilt in anyone else.* As I sat on my chair, I was flooded with all the ways in which I still believed others were guilty. Loved ones, friends, and politicians all came to mind, saddled with the classic ego belief I had laid upon them: *If they were different, then I would be okay.* In other words, I was innocent because someone else was guilty.

I was willing to look at this belief in guilt with my Inner Therapist. I was willing to release the guilt and free those individuals from the burden I was laying on them.

And guess what: the physical symptom that had been present for days completely disappeared. This was a powerful learning moment, when I saw how my unconscious guilt was fueling fear and how I could look at that guilt with my Inner Therapist in order to heal it.

Deeply Questioning Our Beliefs and Fears

If you would be a real seeker after truth,
it is necessary that at least once in your life you doubt,
as far as possible, all things.

René Descartes

The second way that we can become aware of our unconscious fear and guilt is through deeply questioning our beliefs and fears.

Nouk Sanchez, author of *The End of Death*, calls the Course-driven process of questioning our beliefs "radical self-inquiry." The following exercise is inspired by her work.

UNCOVERING UNCONSCIOUS FEAR

1. Write out a two-column list. In the first column, list the things that are important to you, such as loved ones, friends, health, your body, belongings, money, situations, and places.

2. Consider each item on the list and ask yourself, "If I fully surrender to Love and release my own independent desire and sense of control surrounding this thing, what do I fear happening as a result?" In other words, when you think about giving this thing to your Inner Therapist and trusting only in God completely and forever, what fears arise? Be completely honest. You are allowing yourself to articulate any unconscious fear. If something comes up, such as fears of sacrifice, loss, or change, write it down in the second column next to the corresponding item in the first column.

3. Go down your list of fears and concerns. One at a time (and taking your time), invite your Inner Therapist to look at those fears with you. You might say: "Inner Therapist, I admit that I have this fear in my mind. I am willing to give it to you for reinterpretation. I want the miracle, a shift in perception, instead of the fear."

4. Rest in trust that you have begun the process of undoing each fear. If you find a lack of trust arising, be willing to look at that lack of trust with your Inner Therapist, too!

This exercise is important because it shows us not only where we lack trust in God and Love, but also how we may unconsciously associate God and Love with fear, or believe that God is something separate from us. As we become aware of our unconscious fear of Love, we can take it to our Inner Therapist and ask for the miracle instead.

Through the self-questioning in this exercise, I have become aware of the following core beliefs. See if any of them ring true for you:

- I am terrified of the Love of God because I'm afraid I'll lose my sense of being me.
- I am afraid of releasing control, which shows me I don't trust God.
- I believe that God is something outside of me and that God's will is something separate from my own.
- I believe that God might take things away from me, which shows me that I fear God and would rather stay in control myself.

By peeling away the layers of the onion, we progressively uncover and heal all the mistaken thoughts our ego has made until all that's left is our awareness of Love. The ego is terrified of the awareness of Love, though, because it points to the ego's lack of reality.

The good news is that we don't hold a multitude of unconscious beliefs that need healing. There is really only one: the belief that we are separate from God. And the answer to this false belief was given to our minds the instant we thought of it; we just haven't accepted it yet. We never left our Source: in this very moment we are safe at home.

We also don't have to follow fear through all its complexities, spending countless hours analyzing our anxieties and phobias: "It is not necessary to follow fear through all the circuitous routes by which it burrows underground and hides in darkness, to emerge in forms quite different from what it is. Yet it *is* necessary to examine each one as long as you would retain the principle that governs all of them. When you are willing to regard them, not as separate, but as different manifestations of the same idea, and one you do not want, they go together" (ACIM T-15.X.5:1–3).

We believe that we are (and want to be) separate from God. All our fears can be traced back to this core belief, and all fear can be instantly undone if this belief is healed. We can't intellectually heal the unconscious guilt we carry until we allow it to come to the surface by working through the process of undoing and slowly learn to meet the conditions of peace. Healing can happen in an instant, for it is already done.

Mind-Straightening Mantras

- There is no guilt in me.
- There is no guilt in others.
- The belief that I still have problems is my only problem. In truth, I am already perfect. I just haven't accepted that yet.
- I choose to heal.
- Part of my mind has not forgotten the truth of what I really am. I'm willing to get to know this part of my mind again.
- What I focus on grows. If I focus on fear, my awareness of it grows. If I focus on Love, my awareness of it grows. I choose to focus on Love, through my Inner Therapist.

Journal Prompts

- What am I afraid to heal?
- What would life look like without my problems?

Step 10: Don't Fight Yourself: Be a Happy Learner

I've always been a good student and a bit of a perfectionist. I loved getting As in school. So as a Course student, I wanted to aim for the A. When I struggled with the lessons and principles, I decided I was not getting an A. I'd wail, "I'm failing the Course!"

The loving voices of my family reminded me, "You're not failing the Course, you're *doing* the Course!" And the Course itself tells us: "If you find resistance strong and dedication weak, you are not ready. *Do not fight yourself*" (ACIM T-30.I.1:6–7).

When struggling leads you to think you should be anywhere other than where you are, the ego is joining the party again. If you have thoughts like "I should be further along with this than I am," "I should be peaceful," or "I should be getting this by now," you can recognize these as ego judgments. Step back from them, and do the most loving thing you can do for yourself: *allow yourself to be exactly where you are.*

You can't speed up your lessons, skip past them, or ignore them. The only way is *through* them. For instance, for years I tried to hand over the difficulty I felt in speaking up to my father. I didn't want to have any awkward confrontations or to exert the effort to address my feelings with him. I often tried to surrender this challenge with my dad directly to my Inner Therapist, but nothing changed. The pattern of fear surfaced over and over.

It turned out that I needed to learn how to speak up to my dad before I could truly begin to see our relationship differently and truly express love for him. I needed to work some things out on this earthly level.

I realized that I'd tried to take a "spiritual bypass" around this situation rather than do the difficult work of learning how to speak to my dad face to face. Yet that evasion was also a part of my lesson: I learned that bypassing doesn't work. If you feel stuck with an issue, maybe it is something you need to go through in order to learn. And this is okay! Call on your Inner Therapist for help in seeing it differently *while* you go through it. If you forget to ask for help while you are dealing with the situation, ask your Inner Therapist afterward. Allowing ourselves to be exactly where we are and to go through what we need to go through, without feeling guilt, is an extraordinary act of kindness toward ourselves. "The happy learner cannot feel guilty about learning" (ACIM T-14.III.1:1).

We may even try to bypass our feelings. Sometimes, for instance, it seems easier just to take the high road and not express anger. But the first step in healing something is to recognize that it is there. This means feeling our feelings. The Course says that "anger is *never* justified" (ACIM T-30.VI.1:1), but it doesn't say we never feel anger. So if you get angry at someone, allow it. If you feel you need to try to fix a situation out in the world, do it. Once we finally realize that ignoring our feelings or blasting others with anger doesn't work, and trying to fix people or situations "out there" will likely fail, then we'll realize that there is "another way" (ACIM W-pI.33).

Allowing Others to Be Where They Are

I used to get very frustrated with my friend Andrew, a fellow Course student and a serial job quitter, because he often found himself in financial difficulties. Once, when he started complaining about his struggles with his current job, I felt my frustration building. What I wanted to impatiently tell him was "Take your pattern to your Inner Therapist already!" but instead I came out with "This is all somehow coming from you."

"I know, I know!" he responded, then continued with his complaint. My frustration and anger kept building. I wanted to get off the phone. I started doing chores around the house while I listened so that I could at least get something useful done.

Then, suddenly, I remembered a teaching from the Course: the task of the miracle worker is to not get angry at other people's wrong-minded thoughts (ACIM M-18.2:1). This was exactly what was happening; I was irritated with the thought pattern that led Andrew to believe in his own complaint and to believe that he could fix his painful situation without the help of his Inner Therapist. In fact, I was frustrated by my own mistake of deciding that Andrew needed to be "fixed." The instant I realized this, I turned to my Inner Therapist with my feelings and my willingness to heal them. I realized I was the one who needed correction. I could allow Andrew to be where he was in his growth. I felt a burden lift.

Not even a minute later, Andrew stopped complaining and said, "I just heard a small voice inside my head, sounding like your voice, say, 'You need to take this to your Inner Therapist.' I feel okay now. I know what to do. I think I'm ready to get off the phone."

I was blown away. Once I let a miracle come into my mind, the whole picture changed. Andrew got the answer he needed, and it came from within himself. I couldn't have told him what he needed: it had to come from him. And it came because I let healing come into my own mind. We were both exactly where we needed to be for our own growth and learning.

The Question of Medication

Another important point about "being where you are" has to do with medication. According to the Course, "Sometimes the illness has a sufficiently strong hold over the mind to render a person temporarily inaccessible to the Atonement [the undoing of fear]. In this case it may be wise to utilize a compromise approach to mind and body, in which something from the outside is temporarily given healing belief" (ACIM T-2.IV.4:5–6).

In short: take medicine if you need it. There is nothing wrong with doing so: I have relied on it at times. Whether we use modern pharmaceutical medication or alternative treatments doesn't matter: both are equal illusions, both things outside ourselves that we believe can heal us — which can be thought of as "magic" (ACIM W-pI.140.2:2). There is no need to feel guilty about either kind of magic.

But if you choose to take medication, do it with your Inner Therapist. In other words, take the meds while asking your Inner Therapist to take your belief in the medication — as well as your belief in the problem that warrants medication — in exchange for a miracle.

You might be wondering, "Why should I take medication if the world is just an illusion?" or "Why should I bother doing anything healthy at all?" It boils down to this: Hardly any of us truly recognize that our minds are already healed. I still haven't accepted that everything I see and experience is coming from my sleeping split mind or that all healing comes from within. I still believe the cause of healing is outside myself, something that will be acquired "later." And I still believe that I am Corinne. Why? Simply because I still want to play in the separation theme park.

We have all made the material world and our bodies very real. Fall down, and you may bruise your knee. Catch a cold, and you'll sneeze. If we say, "I'm going to stop caring for my body or taking my medication because it's all an illusion," then we're engaging in what is called "level confusion" (ACIM T-2.IV.2:2). We're trying to correct ourselves while relying on the ego as our guide. We're taking over the Inner Therapist's job and trying to undo the false beliefs in our mind alone. And that will get us into trouble, because we haven't truly accepted that the world is an illusion: "Many have chosen to renounce the world while still believing its reality. And they have suffered from a sense of loss, and have not been released accordingly" (ACIM W-pI.155.4:2–3).

We can come to recognize the unreality of the world only through experiences, not through intellectual understanding. Those experiences come in the form of miracles as we allow ourselves to be where we are, and as we take everything to our Inner Therapist. We can take our *beliefs* in medication, in eating kale, drinking organic fresh juice, and eating non-GMO soybeans and offer all of them to our Inner Therapist.

We've made idols out of such things, believing they can "save" us. Our beliefs in healing substances are beliefs in magic, but we can free ourselves by giving them to our Inner Therapist to be transformed. Our Inner Therapist can give us back miracles that demonstrate, in ways we can understand, that we are mind, and that the body is simply a vehicle for learning, one that cannot suffer. The only thing that can really save us is awakening to the fact that we are not these bodies, have not left God, and are not guilty. Our Inner Therapist will prove to us by our own personal experiences that this is so.

So address what you need to address. Take medication if you believe you need it. Get into therapy if you need it. Your Inner Therapist can speak to you through others if you are too blocked to hear your Inner Therapist's Voice yourself.

Learn some self-healing skills. Write a letter to the person you're still angry at (though if you intend to send it, wait at least three days and reread it before sending it to be sure it feels right). Make some changes out there in the world whenever you feel the need. Call on your Inner Therapist while you do these things. And don't feel guilty for going through your experiences. Guilt is just the ego trying to sustain your belief in it. If guilt arises, take it to your Inner Therapist. If you notice that you're being really hard on yourself, go easy and be kinder. You can choose to be a patient and happy learner. Remember that things fall away as we're ready to let them go. You don't have to force anything.

For help with allowing yourself to be where you are and for being a happy learner, enjoy this meditation.

LET'S MEDITATE: BEING A HAPPY LEARNER

This meditation is about fully accepting yourself wherever you are in your journey. If you find yourself thinking that you should be further along on your journey or more spiritually advanced than you are, know that is the voice of the ego. There are no accidents or wrong directions; you are exactly where you need to be right now.

Begin by grounding with three breaths, noticing the full duration of each inhalation and exhalation.

Calling to mind a specific expectation in which you feel something should be different than it is right now, say, "Inner Therapist, I give this outcome that I want to you. I don't know what anything is for."

Notice breathing in and out as you embody the phrase, "I don't know what anything is for." Allow the feeling of *not knowing* to create space and openness and freedom within you.

Breathe through each of the following statements:

- I am willing to be a happy learner.
- I am exactly where I need to be for my own growth and learning.
- Everything that is coming up is an opportunity to bring it to my Inner Therapist.
- I do not know what anything is for.
- I am willing to be a happy learner.

Mind-Straightening Mantras

- I give myself permission to be exactly where I am.
- I do not feel guilty about relying on medication.
- I will not judge myself for the temporary means I need for healing.
- I am willing to look at my belief in the healing power of kale with the Inner Therapist (as I chomp it down).
- I am willing to look at my belief, with my Inner Therapist, that anything outside my mind has healing powers.
- Inner Therapist, heal my perception that I am this body.

Journal Prompt

As attack "is withdrawn from without, there is a strong tendency to harbor it within" (ACIM T-11.IV.4:5). Where do you notice that you are being hard on yourself? Write out the ways you think you need to be different. Look at each one, and as you give it to your Inner Therapist, say, "Inner Therapist, I accept that I am exactly where I need to be for my greatest growth and learning. I give this self-attacking thought to you to be undone."

CHAPTER EIGHT

Peace-Inducing Perception Shifts: Five Things to Think

𝕊𝕩𝕊

*N*ow you know something about the process of moving from anxiety to love. I repeat, *this is a process*. For most of us, change doesn't happen overnight. The more you dedicate yourself to the process, however, the faster it happens. What you focus on comes nearer to you. When you focus on your willingness to remember Love, you begin to remember it.

Overcoming anxiety requires significant shifts of perception. We cannot make these perception shifts by ourselves because we are accustomed to yielding to the fearful voice of the ego. We need to ask for the help of the Inner Therapist, who is not separate from us but is outside the ego thought system, and who works only by invitation.

This chapter and the next one describe some of the internal

shifts that I had to make to heal my mistaken belief in anxiety. The process is highly individualized, so you will have to decide for yourself which shifts you need to make, and in what order. Don't be surprised when your direction shifts. On some days, certain ideas were like healing medicine for me, and on other days they felt inert. That doesn't matter. What *does* matter is your focus on your Inner Therapist. Every day is different because "complexity is of the ego" (ACIM T-15.IV.6:2), and the ego has entrenched itself in our seemingly separate minds.

Through practicing these shifts and working with our Inner Therapist, we are learning to remember who we really are by removing the blocks that we have interposed between peace and our awareness of it. Already, in this very moment, "peace is an attribute *in* you" (ACIM T-2.I.5:8). The more we come to know and experience the truth about ourselves, the more unlikely anxiety becomes.

You can use any one of these *peace-inducing perception shifts* when you're feeling fear. Find the one that is the perfect medicine for you at the time. You can practice them in order or in any sequence that resonates with you.

Shift 1: This Is Happening Because It Is an Opportunity for Me to Grow

When you're in the thick of anxiety or any painful situation, it is all-encompassing, dark, and terrifying. You hate it, and you wish it would go away. But when that kind of situation arises, it's time to recognize what's happening and not run away from it. You don't have to like it: you just have to acknowledge it. Anxiety is an opportunity to grow, if you are mindful of it.

If you're kicking and screaming, you're only going to create more anxiety and pain for yourself. That is the ego keeping you in ego. Instead, be willing to work with your anxiety rather than against it. Anxiety can be a harsh teacher — like the grade school instructors my dad told me about who whacked their students' knuckles with a ruler — but it's still a teacher if you view it as such.

I look at most situations in my life as opportunities to grow. Anxiety is a call to awaken. Can you allow it then, to be your teacher? To gain the freedom to move through a current challenge, you have to be willing to let go of how things used to be. We can't go back, but we can go through and come out the other side with a new awareness. Looking at this process as growth can prevent us from having to ask, "Why is this happening to me?" Anxiety is happening because it is your perfect teacher, giving you an opportunity to grow.

Anxiety is a great indicator of how closely we're identified with the ego. If you are feeling anxious, you can be sure that you are lost in ego. And so it is time to choose again. "Discomfort is aroused only to bring the need for correction into awareness" (ACIM T-2.V.7:8).

Anxiety causes great discomfort. It is not our Inner Therapist (or God) who arouses this discomfort, but our identification with a false self. So when we feel anxiety, it's a sign that we need the willingness to recognize that somehow, somewhere, we've made a choice that led to pain.

This prayer in the Course is a perfect reset button for me:

I must have decided wrongly, because I am not at peace.
I made the decision myself, but I can also decide otherwise.
I want to decide otherwise, because I want to be at peace.
I do not feel guilty, because the Holy Spirit will undo all the
    consequences of my wrong decision if I will let Him.
I choose to let Him, by allowing Him to decide for God
    for me. (ACIM T-5.VII.6:7–11)

Let's look at this prayer line by line:

I must have decided wrongly, because I am not at peace.

Anytime I do not feel peaceful, *I am the one* who has chosen wrongly. I've made a choice somehow to be in the wrong-mindedness of the ego. And that's the whole problem; no one else causes my distress.

I made the decision myself, but I can also decide otherwise.

I made the decision *myself*. And whenever I'm choosing alone, I'm deciding without my Inner Therapist. That's the recipe for anxiety and fear. Thank goodness I have the power to choose again!

I want to decide otherwise, because I want to be at peace.

This line asserts our willingness: we *want* to make a different decision that will bring us peace instead of pain.

I do not feel guilty, because the Holy Spirit will undo all the consequences of my wrong decision if I will let Him.

The consequences of every screwup, mistake, and fearful thought can be undone right now *if* I turn everything over to my Inner Therapist (the Holy Spirit). There is no need to feel guilty about whatever went wrong. The consequences are not karmic: instead, they are what we experience when we choose the ego — that is, fear — as our teacher. If we've made decisions that bring the consequence of fear, that can be undone the moment we allow our Inner Therapist to step in.

I choose to let Him, by allowing Him to decide for God for me.

We can let our Inner Therapist undo the consequences of our wrong decisions only *if we let it choose for God on our behalf.* We don't know how to choose for God, because we are truly confused about who we are and what God is. But our Inner Therapist is the part of our mind that knows how.

This prayer is enormously comforting, because even though we've made a mistake that might cause us pain, we can trust that it can be undone in an instant. Just when I was so anxious that I thought it would seriously affect my health, I remembered this prayer and felt relieved. My Inner Therapist could undo all the consequences of my wrong decision!

Success is guaranteed. Once we embark on our path, the outcome is certain. And if our success is guaranteed, then we are heading toward peace. We can always take comfort in that. The blocks we've built to Love are seemingly painful indeed, but we're learning to remove those blocks. So keep your mind focused on the goal, which is "the attainment and the keeping of the state of peace" (ACIM T-24.In.1:1). We're going to make it. That is guaranteed by Love. So give it a try.

The Course suggests that we're as safe now as we were before the separation seemingly happened, as we will be when the seeming separation is over. How awesome is that?

Mind-Straightening Mantras

- Will I go through fear to love? Yes, I will.
- This is an opportunity for me to grow.
- I am not going crazy, I am learning to become more sane.

- Inner Therapist, please choose for Love for me, because I don't know how!

📖 Journal Prompt

How do you feel about your anxiety? Does it make you angry? Afraid? Can you be willing to see it as a teacher? Write until you can recognize that your challenges are an opportunity to grow.

Shift 2: I Am Not a Body

My mind is not in my body; my body is in my mind.

Course study-group participant

You are not [*your name here*].

Shifting from anxiety to love is about coming to know your true identity, which is not based in a body. You are not your personality. You are not your self-concept. You are not this clay garment. All these identities derive from the ego.

All our problems stem from a bad case of mistaken identity — a "great amnesia," as the Course calls it (ACIM T-19.IV.D.3:4). We have forgotten who we truly are because our sense of self seems to be fused with the body. To really make progress with undoing fear, the Course tells us, "the insignificance of the body must be an acceptable idea" (ACIM M-5.II.3:12).

If we're constantly focused on the body, trying to make it healthier and prettier, then we're only going to get so far in our spiritual growth. We don't have to fully accept the body as meaningless; we just have to be open to the idea that it might be.

My anxiety about my health has been triggered more than once by an abnormally heavy menstrual period (sorry, guys: if this grosses you out, imagine how I felt). I feared I was bleeding to death, even though this was completely irrational. My body seemed oh-so-real at these times. In working with my Inner Therapist, I got in touch with the idea that I am afraid of my own body because I believe it can hurt me. This is a perfect example of making the body into a *cause*, rather than what it really is — an *effect* of the mind.

If the body is a cause, it can do things to me: make me feel unwell, give me panic attacks, or even end my life. No one would argue that it does not, in fact, do these things. But this is upside-down perception.

Our mind is a cause, because it is dreaming of separation. The body is an effect of our desire to be separate. So, again, our mind is not in our body; *our body is in our mind*. And there is no cause of suffering that can come from outside our own mind, because the sleeping part of our Child Mind is the dreamer of the dream.

Although we might be able to wrap our heads around this intellectually, we can't understand true cause and effect unless we have experiences that show them to us. To have such an experience, all you need is the willingness to consider that you might be wrong about the body.

Through my own willingness, I experienced this teaching. My husband and I were recently working on our laptops on our back porch, and he lit a citronella candle to keep the mosquitoes away. Sitting downwind of it, I soon noticed my sinuses starting to ache. "Uh-oh," I thought. "This better not trigger a sinus headache." But it did. Within thirty minutes, I was writhing in pain. When I get these headaches, they last for at least a day.

I noticed anger arise. Why did my husband have to light that stupid candle? As the urge to blame and attack arose in me, I also noticed that I was placing the cause of my pain outside myself: "The candle caused my headache, dammit."

Fortunately, I felt prompted to go sit quietly on my couch. Something inside me clicked. "This is a trap," I realized. "An ego setup. And I'm actually recognizing it. I'm willing to examine this with the Inner Therapist as my guide." As I muttered, "This is a trap" to myself, this sequence of thoughts rushed forward: "My sleeping split mind, which is believing in the ego, is behind this. It has nothing to do with the candle. This situation is a trap, set by the ego, to prove its reality. It doesn't want me to question this situation. It just wants my sleeping split mind to keep pumping belief into the ego. After all, if I'm in pain, there is no better evidence to 'prove' that I must be a body. Pain is the ego's best strategy to prevent me from questioning the situation."

In the ego's closed loop of logic, this is what appears to have happened: my husband lit the candle (cause), so I got a sinus headache (effect). So I was right to be angry and fearful, blame my husband, and conclude that I was an innocent victim.

Yet, as the Course says, "The secret of salvation is but this: that you are doing this unto yourself" (ACIM T-27.VIII.10:1). With a miracle, I could see the ego's closed loop for what it was: a trick.

What really happened was this: My sleeping split Child Mind (the cause of the dream) was pumping belief into the ego, because it was afraid to look back to Love. The ego wanted to prove that I must be a body and that this world must be real, because its existence depends on that belief. Since ideas don't leave their source, the thought of pain was coming from the sleeping part of my mind, not the citronella candle!

So I decided, "I take responsibility for this. I'll look at it with my Inner Therapist." For an instant, I felt Love's presence with me; I was not alone in my living room.

And then the headache evaporated. I felt a mild sensation in my sinuses for about an hour, but I knew the healing had happened and that my body would catch up to my mind's decision to place cause and effect in their proper place. And that is exactly what happened. The headache was gone without medicine, much more quickly than usual, without any physical or medical intervention on my part. All it took was my willingness to recognize that I was the cause of this dream.

The skeptic in you might have another explanation: physical irritants cause physical reactions, so if you remove the irritant, the reaction will stop. If we believe we are a body, it is true that we are subject to the laws of the world. But that's also the ego's trap to convince you that the external world is real. "Nothing can hurt you unless you give it the power to do so" (ACIM T-20.IV.1:1). By recognizing that the cause of my trouble was coming from my mind, I no longer allowed an external circumstance to have power over me.

The Course's teachings on cause and effect go even deeper, for there is truly only one cause and effect. God, or Love, is the Cause, and we are its Effects. You can take comfort that you did not create yourself but were created by perfect Love, and you remain exactly as you were created. This crazy dream we *think* we are in has not changed our reality in the slightest bit. "I am not a body. I am free. For I am still as God created me" (ACIM W-pI.201).

When we realize that we are "still as God created" us, we can begin to see the body as a means of waking up from this dream. We tend to think of the body as an end versus a means. It gives us moments of pleasure between almost constant attempts to avoid or diminish pain. That's because the ego uses the body to stay separate from Love. When you give the body to the Inner Therapist's purpose, it becomes the means for awakening, to be "gently laid by" when it has fulfilled its usefulness (ACIM Preface, "What It Says").

To begin to learn that you are not a body, simply be willing to see it differently. Give that willingness to your Inner Therapist and ask for an experience that teaches you that you are not a body. This is different from asking God to help your body, or another person's body. Let's face it: When you ask God for help, don't you usually have the identity of your body (or someone else's body) in mind? The real changes start to happen when we become willing to loosen this fusion with our bodies: "I am not [*your name here*]." Prayer becomes "Let me see the truth that I am not a body" instead of "Please make this turn out the way I want, so my body (or someone else's body) will be okay!" Each time you turn to your Inner Therapist, ask for the truth to be shown to you, and be willing to learn that you do not know it. Become willing to live differently, with a focus on truth rather than a focus on your bodily identity.

Mind-Straightening Mantras

- Teach me the right perception of the body, I am willing to learn.
- I am not [*your name here*].
- I did not create myself.
- My body is a means, not an end.
- My body is an effect of my mind, not a cause.
- "I am spirit" (ACIM W-pI.97).

Journal Prompt

Do you believe that your body can hurt you and cause your life to end? How are you afraid of your body? List all your body-based beliefs and be willing to give each one to your Inner Therapist for reinterpretation. Trust that your perception will shift instantly the moment you are ready.

Shift 3: The Ego Has the Issues, Not Me!

We can easily feel overwhelmed by all our "issues" that we think need healing. We may struggle with anxiety, depression, codependency, addiction, loneliness, lack, illness, conflict, or any combination thereof. It seems like a lot to heal.

Ready for some good news? The ego has the issues, not you! The ego is only a belief in a part of your mind, even though it likes to tell you it's *all* of your mind and that you have nowhere else to go for love, support, and wisdom. I talk about myself in the third person here, but please substitute your name for mine. I also focus on what has been my primary "problem" in life — anxiety — but please substitute your own.

"Corinne has anxiety because the construct of Corinne is an ego identity. I am learning, however, that I am not Corinne, and my true identity is at perfect peace."

Rather than fixing anxiety so that I can feel okay, I'm learning how to let go of my identity as Corinne and wake up to the truth of who I am. As I let go of the identity of Corinne, the anxiety issues fall away. I still look the same to others, but the source of my identity is now coming from the Love within. I look at least a little different, because I smile more.

When I refer to "letting go" of my identity as Corinne, I am not referring to dying. Contemplating suicide or death does not allow us to transcend the ego. We have to learn to transcend our identity in this world *now*, by loving our way out of the separation theme park with our Inner Therapist's help. Nothing is accomplished through death: peace comes from awakening. As the Course says, "'Rest in peace' is a blessing for the living, not the dead" (ACIM T-8.IX.3:5).

Rest comes from waking up. The ego has the issues; you, however, are still perfect and whole, and you have simply mistaken your ego body for your self. You remain unchanged in what you are, despite the crazy rides you've been on in the separation theme park. As you learn to remove the blocks you've built to knowing Love, you come to remember that Love is actually who you are.

Then peace inevitably returns, because you are now meeting the conditions of peace.

Whenever the ego feels like it is really acting up, try experimenting with the following meditation.

LET'S MEDITATE: QUIETING THE EGO

This meditation is for quieting the hyperactive ego, which is vigilant on behalf of itself but is not looking out for your true peace. The ego is nothing to fear; it cannot hurt you. It depends only on your belief in it. When you actively get mad at the voice of the ego (and the anxiety habit that comes with it), you're pouring the fuel of judgment onto the ego's flame, thus keeping it burning. The voice therefore gets louder. Instead, let's practice embodying kindness and facing the ego's fearful voice without judgment.

Take a deep breath and bring your attention to your willingness to think of the ego voice differently. The ego voice is not your voice. The ego is not actually part of you. It is a false identification that we're learning how to detach from. Allow these words of gratitude to sink into your mind and heart:

Ego, thank you for your counsel in trying to keep me safe. I hear you loud and clear. Thank you for your hypervigilance in trying to protect me. Thank you for the role you've played in helping me remember that there is another way. I'm done with your fearful voice now, because there is a gentler path I'm willing to follow. I want to be truly happy. So I'm not going to listen to you anymore.

Next, allow these phrases to sink into your being:

I am willing to not judge myself.
I am willing to accept myself.
I am willing to accept my feelings.
I am willing to love myself as I am.
I am willing to allow myself to be where I am.

Take a deep breath in and out. Again, repeat these phrases, fully dropping into the feelings of these words:

I release all self-judgment.
I accept myself completely.
I accept my feelings.
I love myself as I am.
I allow myself to be where I am.

Take another deep breath in and out. Allow these words to fill your mind:

I am safe.
I am at peace.
I am loved.

Rest in the kindness of these words for as long as you would like.

 Mind-Straightening Mantras

• [*Your name here*] will always have issues. As I loosen my grip on this identity, issues fall away.

- I am not an ego.
- I am willing to know my Self.
- There is a deep part of me that is always at peace, even though the surface part of me feels pain.
- Since "the ego becomes strong in strife" (ACIM T-5. III.8:8), I choose to not judge myself.

📖 Journal Prompt

Think of a problem you currently are struggling with. What is the payoff from holding on to this problem? Get really honest, and be willing to look at your response with your Inner Therapist.

Shift 4: Sickness Is of the Mind, Not the Body

This shift derives from the shift of "I am not a body." Because the body is an *effect* of your mind, the body can't be the source of sickness. It does nothing and is wholly neutral; sickness is actually of the mind.

Wanting to be a separate self means that we choose to perceive ourselves outside our natural state of Oneness. Because of this false perception, our minds are unwell. But sickness and healing have nothing to do with "negative thinking" or "positive thinking." Each has to do with which teacher we choose to follow. Our collective choice to side with the ego makes us vulnerable to sickness; our choice to turn all our perceptions and beliefs over to the Inner Therapist leads to healing the mind.

Because both negative and positive thoughts can come from ego, a belief that only negative thinking causes sickness cannot hold true. Negative thinking certainly isn't going to make you feel fabulous, but getting worried that you're going to make yourself sick because of negative thoughts is only fueling the ego. Instead, it is the identification with the ego that brings pain and suffering.

Remember this key point we've mentioned before: we're not going to stop having negative thoughts, but we're going to have "none that we would keep" (ACIM T-15.IV.9:1–2). Any consequences of our wrong-minded thinking can be undone in an instant by turning to our Inner Therapist. This is why you don't have to worry about your negative thoughts. You have the means to let those thoughts be exchanged for miracles. You can trust your Inner Therapist to transform them.

Also, there is no need to feel guilty if you are sick. Sickness is simply the ego presenting you with seemingly strong evidence that you are a body. Our task is to ask for a different perception, because our Inner Therapist is capable of "seeing past appearances" (ACIM W-pI.92.4:1). Under the light of our Inner Therapist, sickness can be given a new purpose as a divine opportunity to heal the mind.

If we want to heal, we have to look to the mind and learn how to see the body properly. As you know by now, we cannot do this alone: "When the ego tempts you to sickness do not ask the Holy Spirit to heal the body, for this would merely be to accept the ego's belief that the body is the proper aim of healing. Ask, rather, that the Holy Spirit teach you the right *perception* of the body, for perception alone can be distorted. Only perception can be sick, because only perception can be wrong" (ACIM T-8.IX.1:5–7).

To ask for a physical ailment to be healed affirms your mistaken belief in a body. If we look to the body to heal, we might succeed in plugging up a hole in a leaky pipe, but the pain of the separation will break through somewhere else (remember the difference between "fixing" and "healing" a problem). We must learn how to properly perceive the body. We must want to heal the mind.

Your body is simply a vehicle to learn the lesson that you are *not* a body, whether you happen to be sick or well. Your body is separate from you. It is a learning device for the mind. The proper use of the body is to let the Inner Therapist communicate through us to other vehicles (bodies) and to learn that our identity does not lie in it. When we assign other roles to it that it cannot fulfill, it becomes vulnerable to sickness. For instance, if we try to use the body as bait to catch another body, to get richer, or to become more special than other bodies, we're misusing it. These are all means of upholding our belief in the separation. We will therefore be susceptible to sickness, suffering, and death.

> The body is in need of no defense. This cannot be too often emphasized. It will be strong and healthy if the mind does not abuse it by assigning it to roles it cannot fill, to purposes beyond its scope, and to exalted aims which it cannot accomplish. (ACIM W-pI.135.7:1–3)

> These are the thoughts in need of healing, and the body will respond with health when they have been corrected and replaced with truth. This is the body's only real defense. (ACIM W-pI.135.10:1–2)

To the ego, the body is a separation device, and it remains the ego's ally until we truly give its purpose over to our Inner Therapist. Then the body becomes a learning and communication device, and it becomes healthy because we perceive it properly. If the body appears to remain sick, we take this appearance to our Inner Therapist and ask for help in accepting the fact that we are whole. Every circumstance is a chance to look at our unconscious beliefs with our Inner Therapist.

Healing comes when we work with our Inner Therapist to learn that we are not separate, and not a body. We still use our body to relate to other people, go to work, and do our daily tasks, but the meaning of everything we do becomes different. Be willing to look to your Inner Therapist instead of to your body for reassurance. You were created in perfect Love, and you remain completely unchanged.

When you get stuck in fear about your own body, experiment with the following meditation.

LET'S MEDITATE:
RELEASING WORRY ABOUT YOUR BODY

This is a meditation for times when you get stuck in fear about your body. The fear could be related to being sick or unwell in some way, worried about aging, or stressed about bodily harm. Whatever the fear, this meditation will help you shift fearful perceptions back to peace.

Begin by noticing the breath, sensing the full duration of each inhalation and exhalation. We can use the breath as an anchor to the present moment. The present moment is where your healing Inner Therapist abides, and where peace is.

Next, bring to mind your specific fear. Notice where you feel the fear in your body and how strongly it wants to capture your attention. This fear is of the ego, offering to keep your attention away from the truth of what you really are: Love. Would you accept the ego's "gift" of fear over peace?

Let the power of these words sink into your being:

"Sickness does not exist in the Mind of God, and so the appearance of sickness cannot be the truth."

With that thought, take a breath of relief, inhaling and exhaling.

Name your specific fear in this statement: "This fearful thought of [*my fear*] does not exist in the Mind of God, and so it cannot be true. God does not know sickness, and so it must be a false perception in my mind."

Remember that healing comes from the mind. It has nothing to do with the body. The body is wholly neutral.

With each inhalation, say to yourself with conviction: "Above all else, I want my perception to be healed."

And with each exhalation, say to yourself with conviction: "Inner Therapist, teach me to think like you."

Remember that what you really are cannot die, cannot be sick, cannot be hurt, and cannot suffer. If you are afraid of any of these things or are suffering in any way, you can be certain that you are simply misperceiving. And you can choose again.

Mind-Straightening Mantras

- Inner Therapist, I am willing to look to you for reassurance, rather than to my body.
- Teach me the right perception of the body.
- "Straighten my mind, my Father. It is sick" (ACIM W-pII.347.1:2–3).
- I want my perception to be healed.
- I want my mind, more than my body, to be healed.

Journal Prompt

What feelings and thoughts does this shift bring up? Does fear arise in any form? If so, write it out and look at it with your Inner Therapist.

Shift 5: Sickness Is a Defense against the Truth

We have many forms of defense against the truth within our-selves. Anxiety is a defense against the truth. Depression is a de-fense against the truth. Addiction and pain in any form are defenses against the truth.

The ego puts up these defenses because the suffering they bring draws our attention away from Love and toward the ego. The purpose of any kind of discomfort is to keep us believing that we are our bodies: the ego shrieks, "See! You *can* be hurt! You *are* this body! You know this is real, because it hurts!" And because it hurts so much, we become overwhelmed and do not look beyond our suffering, which is what the ego wants. The purpose of all sickness is to keep us believing that this world is real and that we really are separate from our Loving Source.

I have used anxiety to defend against the truth. Anxiety is all-consuming, and it feels more real than Love. This makes the ego happy. The ego is afraid that if I listened to my Inner Thera-pist, I'd abandon it, which is true enough!

Feelings like anxiety, pain, and sickness are nothing more than the ego dangling a shiny token in front of your nose, hoping you will take the bait. If you do, you'll be convinced that you are a body and that this world is real. All pain is a form of temptation. The ego presents you with temptations like anxiety because it is confident that it can hook your attention with them.

Pain consumes our attention. Yet there is nothing stron-ger than Love. It seems so easy to go down the path of a well-entrenched ego habit of painful thoughts. But we are now developing a habit of miracle working instead of a habit of suffer-ing. The Course tells us, "You can be as vigilant against the ego's dictates as for them" (ACIM T-4.IV.4:2).

At some point you have to decide, "I don't want the old habit anymore," and nurture the new habit of turning to your Inner Therapist whenever the painful allure of the old habit arises. This is where we need to develop vigilance.

There is a passage from the Course that I use whenever I experience pain or extreme fear. I use it when I see something terrible, too, like the time I hit a squirrel with my car. "Take this from me and look upon it, judging it for me. Let me not see it as a sign of sin and death, nor use it for destruction. Teach me how not to make of it an obstacle to peace, but let You [Inner Therapist] use it for me, to facilitate its coming" (ACIM T-19.IV.C.i.11:8–10).

I give the Inner Therapist what I see because otherwise I will use it as a witness that death and sickness are real. My Inner Therapist can see past appearances for me. When I give these sights and feelings to my Inner Therapist to judge for me, I have experiences that reinforce my decision for peace.

Ultimately, we develop vigilance only to learn that vigilance is unnecessary, because the truth is already here. We simply are learning to accept Love again. "Your vigilance is the sign that you *want* Him to guide you. Vigilance does require effort, but only until you learn that effort itself is unnecessary. You have exerted great effort to preserve what you made because it was not true. Therefore, you must now turn your effort against it. Only this can cancel out the need for effort, and call upon the being which you both *have* and *are*. This recognition is wholly without effort since it is already true and needs no protection" (ACIM T-6.V.C.10:3–8).

Mind-Straightening Mantras

- Anxiety is a defense against the truth. I want to learn how *not* to defend against the truth. I am willing to look at this with my Inner Therapist.

- If I defend against the truth, I do not feel guilty, because I allow myself to be where I am.
- Inner Therapist, decide for me. I trust it is done.
- If "sickness is a defense against the truth," I'm willing to learn how to allow the truth to return to my awareness instead (ACIM W-pI.136).

Journal Prompt

Think about something you are currently dealing with. Say the above prayer as you hold the issue in your mind: "Take this from me and look upon it, judging it for me." What rises up in you? Do you feel a genuine willingness to let your Inner Therapist judge it for you? Write a few paragraphs about what you notice and touch your willingness to let your Inner Therapist judge for you.

CHAPTER NINE

Peace-Inducing Perception Shifts: Five More Things to Think

❧

We're spending a lot of time on the issue of shifting perceptions because this process is so important for miracle working. Changing the way you see things is a miracle, because it changes what you see in the world as well as how you're seeing it.

Most people probably think miracles are beyond their power, performed unpredictably by a faraway God who may or may not be listening to our prayers. That can make our prayers anxiety-provoking, because it places God outside ourselves and puts us in a passive position of hoping to receive God's blessing only if we are lucky or special. What we've learned, though, is that God is Love and *only* Love. We are *always* blessed, and God is within us. Miracles are therefore a choice. It is our decision to allow fear to be undone in our mind in order to remember our Oneness with our Loving Source and with one another. When we remember our Oneness, anxiety cannot exist. Through our willingness to experience shifts in perception, we learn that miracles are natural, instantaneous, and available to us right now.

Let's explore five more healing shifts in perception to make room for unstoppable inner peace.

Shift 6: The Ego Has No Power over Me

I used to get really freaked out by the idea that the more I turned to Love, the more the ego would roar at me and whip me back into place. I am well aware that the ego will pull out any evidence to "prove" to us that we are not of Love. Some have referred to this as an "ego backlash."

Although the ego is perfectly capable of having hissy fits and doing what it can to get our attention, we do not have to fear it or a backlash the slightest bit. First and foremost, we need to acknowledge that fearing the ego is *fueling* the ego. By fearing the ego's tantrums, we give it power and make it seem more real.

Think of a giant dancing balloon figure, like the ones you often see outside stores, powered by a fan so that the figure whips back and forth with the force of the wind inside it. This crazy balloon guy represents the ego: a hollow shell filled with nothing. It seems scary only when it is puffed up with moving air. That moving air represents our belief. We are the ones that choose to blow the air into the balloon figure, and by doing so we end up terrorizing ourselves. We do not have to do this: "The ego depends solely on your willingness to tolerate it" (ACIM T-9.VIII.6:1).

As our trust in our Inner Therapist deepens, we start turning off the fan (our belief) that inflates the compelling balloon figure (the ego), choosing instead to see the Love that permeates everything. This choice deflates the ego. It loses power, and it has no shape or force of its own. The Course points out that we become "invulnerable" when we do not protect the ego (ACIM T-4.VII.8:3).

Not protecting the ego is like not blowing air into the balloon. By being willing to question and look at our beliefs with our Inner Therapist, by being willing to not believe the picture of the external world, and to deciding that we know nothing, we allow the ego to be deflated and collapsed. It quite literally has *no* power to hurt us.

Mind-Straightening Mantras

- The ego is nothing to fear.
- The ego has no power over me.
- I am safe because I choose to not protect the ego.
- I am willing to be completely free of the belief in ego.
- I am willing to not place my belief in the ego, and instead I am willing to place it in Love.

Journal Prompt

Ask yourself, "Do I have any fear of the ego in my mind? What are some things I am afraid that the ego is capable of?" Write out any fears you can think of, and be willing to look at each fear with your Inner Therapist. Conclude your journal entry with a statement of your freedom: "The ego has no power over me."

Shift 7: I Don't Have to Master My Anxiety or Fears: I Can Find Peace by Mastering Love

Attempting the mastery of fear is useless. In fact, it asserts the power of fear by the very assumption that it need be mastered. The true resolution rests entirely on mastery through love.

ACIM T-2.VII.4:2–4

What a relief to know we do not have to master our fears! This is a really important shift. We can waste a lot of time trying to work on our fears, but in truth we don't have to "clean up shop" and conquer anxiety on our own. All we have to do is learn mastery through love, and then the anxiety falls away.

We learn mastery through love by letting the Inner Therapist choose for God *for* us, because we don't know how to do it otherwise. None of us can be our own Inner Therapist. Although it is part of us, it fully remembers Love. Since we have accepted the ego into our minds, we have forgotten the Love of God (big time). Our Inner Therapist remembers it for us. Because we have made our own fear, we have to be willing to bring it to the light of Love to be undone. Fear is only a construct of the ego, and it is unknown by God.

It is not only difficult feelings like fear that we can bring to the Inner Therapist. To truly heal, we need to bring everything in our lives to our Inner Therapist. The ego is insidious: "There is no area of your perception that it has not touched" (ACIM T-14.I.2:7). This means that the ego is not just involved in what is painful: it has a stake in what we consider good as well.

The ego will use anything to reinforce its specialness. To work toward mastery of love, practice giving *everything* to your Inner Therapist to be used on behalf of truth. I make it part of my regular practice to give everything in my life that I love to my Inner Therapist. I make a list of everything that is meaningful to me, or that I believe provides safety, and one by one I toss those things into my Inner Therapist's arms. I say,

Inner Therapist, I give you:
My husband
My body
My health

My mind

My family

My house

My business

My money

Be specific in naming what you love. For instance, instead of saying, "I give you my relationships," say, "I give you my spouse," "I give you my partner," "I give you my son (or daughter)," "I give you my mom (or dad)."

It's important to be specific because otherwise it is likely that the ego will misuse these things by using them on behalf of its goal of separation, and that goal brings pain. For instance, the ego will use money to tell you that your safety lies in it and that if you don't have any, you will be in trouble. When you give money to your Inner Therapist for repurposing, it becomes something neutral. You learn that your true safety comes not from money but from Love, and what you need will be provided. Our Inner Therapist uses whatever we give it to promote our waking up and remembering Love. When I go through this laundry list and give over everything to my Inner Therapist, including the things I love and any fears that may be present, I get a sense of peace that is better than anything this world could give me.

If you find yourself reluctant to give something to your Inner Therapist, pause and ask why. Chances are that this resistance indicates an unconscious belief that you'll be asked to sacrifice something. This is never the case. God asks no sacrifice: only the ego does. It is important to look at any fear that comes up with your Inner Therapist by your side.

One way of mastering love that resonates with me comes from a prayer of Hoʻoponopono, a Hawaiian method of healing, which I learned about from the book *Zero Limits*, by Joe Vitale and Ihaleakala Hew Len. This particular prayer uses four phrases that evoke the Course for me. You can repeat it silently in any stressful situation:

I love you.
I'm sorry.
Please forgive me.
Thank you.

Each phrase contains deep meaning behind the words. My Course-inspired interpretation of each one is:

- "I love you": This is a statement of recognition that there is no difference between Love and myself. I joyously acknowledge that I remain as Love created me.
- "I'm sorry": This is a statement of radical responsibility. I've misused my creative will and made a mess. I take complete responsibility for what is coming from my mind.
- "Please forgive me": This request is self-fulfilling, like asking for a miracle. We have already been forgiven because we have never left our Source. Think of forgiveness as "for giving" to our Inner Therapist. I am willing to give this stressful situation to my Inner Therapist in order to receive a miracle instead.
- "Thank you": It is done!

These four simple phrases can help you pursue mastery of love. It is a huge relief to realize that you do not have to master anxiety. Anxiety falls away, because it is not who you are.

Mind-Straightening Mantras

- I cannot be my own Inner Therapist. It won't work!
- I allow my Inner Therapist to choose for Love *for* me.
- I don't have to master anxiety. I am willing to learn mastery of love.
- I give my life to my Inner Therapist, because my Inner Therapist knows better than I do.

Journal Prompt

Make a list of everything that is important to your identity in this world, including beliefs, feelings, and relationships. After your list is complete, give each thing to your Inner Therapist. If you notice fear, pause, name the fear, and be willing to look at it with your Inner Therapist. Ask for a miracle instead. Remember that your Inner Therapist will *never* ask for sacrifice.

Shift 8: I Don't Know What Is Best for Me, and I Don't Know What Makes Me Happy

This may initially sound like an expression of confusion and discontent. But with radical rethinking, it becomes a statement of joy and freedom. We often get caught up in thinking we know what will make us happy, what we should believe, or what everything is for. The truth is, we know nothing. Zilch!

If we think we know, it's like we're holding a teacup full to the brim with tea. The tea represents our beliefs and perceptions. There is no room for our Inner Therapist to fill our cup with new perceptions, because we hang on to what we already have. It becomes our task to dump our stale tea so that our Inner Therapist can fill our cup with miracles instead. The miracles point to the truth that we are the dreamers of this dream.

Recently I was scheduled for an individual appointment with a yoga teacher, but when I arrived, it turned out the teacher was double booked. I opted to be the one to leave the studio and was willing to not judge the situation. I adopted the attitude of "I do not know what anything is for" (ACIM W-pI.25), although I noted that I felt disappointed and a bit annoyed. I felt those feelings, then handed them to my Inner Therapist. Shortly after I left, there was a torrential downpour, and the street where I'd been parked was flooded. The woman who stayed for the appointment, who had a large SUV, barely made it off the street with the water lapping at the bottom of her car. Had I been the one to stay, my beloved little Honda Fit wouldn't have stood a chance in the floodwater.

We often get into trouble because we ascribe false meanings to our experiences. For instance, I might notice a particular bodily symptom and ascribe meaning to it — usually that I'm dying. This causes excessive anxiety. If I were to remain in a place of "not knowing," I'd spare myself a lot of pain.

But not knowing freaks many of us out. We want to know, we want to control, and we want to plan. If saying "I don't know" scares you, remind yourself that your Inner Therapist *does* know, and your Inner Therapist is not separate from you. Your Inner Therapist knows the truth of who you are, is wholly reliable, and can always be counted on. And your Inner Therapist is part of your very own Right Mind.

When you know that you know nothing, you can let miracles unfold.

Mind-Straightening Mantras

- I don't know!
- Instead of deciding what everything means, I let my Inner Therapist tell me.

- I can "learn to lay all judgment aside" and ask only what I really want "in every circumstance" (ACIM M-4.I.7:8).
- I'm willing to dump out my perceptions. Inner Therapist, give me new ones!

Journal Prompt

Complete the following sentences. Fill in the blanks with as many relevant things as you can think of:

I think _____ will make me happy.
I think _____ will make me unhappy.

Look at each of your responses with your Inner Therapist as you remind yourself that you don't truly know what anything is for.

Shift 9: I Am Willing to Release Everything

Thus far, I have not regularly used the word *forgiveness* in this book. Yet I've actually been talking about it all along. It's a key concept in healing our sense of separation from one another and from our Source. It is not something we have to ask for, since we are already safe at home in Love, but it is something we need to practice, because we do not *know* that we are safe at home in Love. Instead, we experience pain and inflict pain because we have accepted the painful thought system of the ego into our minds. This is where the healing needs to happen. We need to forgive ourselves and others through practicing a radical form of forgiveness, which is different from the type of forgiveness we're used to.

Initially it might seem as though forgiveness and anxiety have nothing to do with each other. I believed I was already a forgiving person: I did not hold grudges and was always willing to give others the benefit of the doubt. Yet I still had panic attacks. This is because most of us are accustomed to the ego's plan of forgiveness, which goes something like this: "Tommy was a jerk. That's plain to see. But I decided to take the high road and forgive him anyway."

In this scenario, we believe what our body's eyes have shown us, and then we judge it. We see Tommy as a body — not what he is in truth, which is part of Love and not a body. This way of thinking keeps us fused with our own ego, because we believe that we have been hurt by Tommy's actions.

There is a different way to think about forgiveness, and it involves your Inner Therapist. It goes like this. You acknowledge that your judgment of Tommy comes from the ego, and you call on your willingness to bring what you're experiencing to your Inner Therapist. You may still feel annoyed, and you readily acknowledge those feelings. It's not that you stop having judgmental thoughts: it's that you have none that you would keep. You recognize that somehow this situation is coming from your split mind. Tommy is playing his part perfectly (by being a jerk) to keep you believing that you are a body! So you give your perception of Tommy the Jerk to your Inner Therapist. You ask for the miracle instead, in order to see with your Inner Therapist's vision. And then your peace will return — as well as an improved relationship with Tommy.

Forgiveness means the belief or judgment you hold is *for giving* to your Inner Therapist.

The Inner Therapist's vision shows that what Tommy did doesn't matter, because you can't actually be hurt. The ego can be hurt, but the ego is part of the dream. Tommy isn't Tommy, and you are not who you think you are. The Inner Therapist is in Tommy's mind, just as it is in your mind. In giving your perception of Tommy over to your Inner Therapist, you are allowing the

Inner Therapist in your mind to join with Tommy's. This is how real forgiveness and healing take place.

We cannot see the Love in Tommy by ourselves; we need our Inner Therapist's help. If we try to deny that he was a jerk, we're denying something that we think has really happened. This is an unhelpful form of denial (that is, believing something is real and denying it anyway). True forgiveness means accepting that what you thought happened never really did, because the truth of what we are has remained unchanged. True forgiveness is about seeing what is true within another person, which is Love, and nothing else.

We can do this with every situation that arises in our lives. We can bring everything to our Inner Therapist for its interpretation instead of our own. Forgiving means that we're willing to release everything to our Inner Therapist. We're willing to let go of our fixed ideas and beliefs to make room for an experience of miracles.

One of my favorite prayers demonstrating this radical forgiveness process comes from Nouk Sanchez, the spiritual director of TakeMeToTruth.org:

Holy Spirit [my Inner Therapist],
Please help me to forgive myself
for having unknowingly used [*a person, sickness, pain,
     self-judgment, etc.*]
to attack myself
and to separate from your love, as my Holy Self.

It is always we ourselves who need forgiveness because we've identified with ego and constantly call forth witnesses to the ego's existence. When we use others to keep the Love of God away from ourselves, we attack ourselves. By being willing to forgive ourselves through forgiving others, we can rapidly remove the blocks to our awareness of Love's presence.

Mind-Straightening Mantras

- I am willing to forgive myself.
- I withhold nothing from my Inner Therapist.
- "Let miracles replace all grievances" (ACIM W-pI.78).
- Do I want to be "right" in my judgments or happy that judgment is not up to me? (ACIM T-29.VII.1:9)

Journal Prompt

Think of a person you currently struggle with, someone you have not forgiven. In your journal, write out the prayer on page 135 and include this person's name. Repeat the prayer silently to yourself to allow the words to sink in. Write down whatever arises for you and be willing to look at it with your Inner Therapist.

Shift 10: I Am Willing to Not Believe the Picture and to Find My "Rock" of a New Reality

"Appearances deceive" (ACIM T-30.IV.5:1), yet we can learn *not* to be deceived by what we see (ACIM M-12.6:8). I like thinking of this process as learning to not believe the picture of the world. Our body's eyes do not show us the truth: every single thing we see will one day perish or disappear. If our true reality is eternal, we are certainly not capable of perceiving this truth with our body's eyes. To know the truth that we deny, we must use the spiritual vision of our Inner Therapist.

When I was in the midst of anxiety, I chose to talk about it with a few people I felt guided to confide in, as I knew they could offer me the kind of help I needed. They included my mom, my stepfather, a few fellow Course students, a doctor, and a therapist. I was not looking for sympathy. I knew my anxiety was an error, and I didn't want it strengthened by anyone who would reinforce my belief that I was sick. And so I chose to talk to certain people I regarded as my rocks, who would reinforce my choice for a new reality. I knew they would care for and be kind to me: in their own ways, they would take the ugly picture they were seeing to our Inner Therapist. This was reassuring for me.

There is only one rock that you truly need: your Inner Therapist. Listening to and learning from your Inner Therapist opens up a whole new thought system to you. However, many of us find that having an earthly support system is also necessary.

When my best friend, Julie, was scared that she might be diagnosed with breast cancer, I told her I would be her rock. I told her that when she thought of me, I wanted her to feel that I was holding steady for her: staying grounded, not getting swept into fear, keeping my mind fixed on not believing the picture of fear. She is not a Course student, and that was the best explanation I could offer about what I would do to help her.

To be Julie's rock, I took a breath, listened to her fully, sensed my body (instead of getting swept away into my own thinking), and turned to my Inner Therapist, asking, "Help me see the truth." I responded to Julie with calmness in my voice and reassurance that I was there for her. Rather than reacting with fear by saying or thinking, "Oh no, you poor thing," I brought my mind into a place of confidence that however this situation unfolded, it would be an opportunity for all of us to remember the truth.

I next went to the prayer "Take this from me and look upon it, judging it for me" (ACIM T-19.IV.C.i.11:8). I knew that the only real way to help Julie was to hold steady and keep my mind fixed on my willingness to be shown by my Inner Therapist that this was all an illusion, and that she was not her body. If I saw her body as real, then I would be holding both of us to this illusion of separation. But I could not see past the picture by myself. I needed the Inner Therapist to choose for God *for* me, because I didn't know how by myself.

If you need a rock, though, it doesn't have to be someone who follows *A Course in Miracles*. You can simply ask a friend, a family member, or a therapist to "hold steady" for you. You can ask them to not buy into the fear of what they are seeing, and you can ask them to be willing to see you as the whole and complete Self that you already are. If you feel comfortable doing it, you can even ask them to take what they see to their Inner Therapist.

You can also use an image of a comforting spiritual being to "see" only the truth in you, as described in the following meditation.

LET'S MEDITATE: ROCK MEDITATION

We are already fully healed and safe at home in Love, but we often choose to forget that. To help you remember the truth of who you are, find a picture that represents someone or something who can see only the truth in you. This might be a representation of the Inner Therapist, Jesus, Buddha, an angel, a pet or any other loved one, or any presence whom you can envision seeing you with perfect love. Choose a picture in which the being is looking directly at you, so you can make eye contact with the eyes of the image. If you don't have a physical picture, imagine this being looking directly at you.

This meditation can be practiced with eyes open or closed.

Begin by taking a mindful breath in and out. Notice the rise and fall of the belly as you breathe.

Look into the eyes of this picture and imagine that this being is seeing only the truth in you, using spiritual vision to look straight past what is false. As this being upholds only the truth, it is a "rock" for you.

Allow yourself to fully feel what it is like to have someone uphold only what is true in you. It feels good. Whatever you believe you are struggling with, it can easily fade into the nothingness that it is. Only the love and peace in you are reinforced. Stay with this feeling and let it radiate throughout you as you breathe in and out.

This is how it feels to be the recipient of your Inner Therapist's vision rather than being seen through the body's eyes.

Just as you have imagined that this being is seeing only the truth in you, you can be willing to use your Inner Therapist's vision to see the truth in others as well. Seeing the truth in others helps us see it in ourselves. Say to yourself, "I am willing to see the light in others, for it reflects the light in me. I am willing to see this light in myself."

Mind-Straightening Mantras

- There is a deep part of me that is at peace, even though the surface part of me feels pain.
- I will not believe the picture of fear.
- Inner Therapist, please choose Love for me, because I don't know how!
- I am willing to see the light in others, for it reflects the light in me.

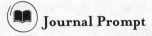 **Journal Prompt**

Who might you ask to be your rock? Who do you feel comfortable confiding in? Ask your Inner Therapist, get quiet, and wait for the answer to come in some form you will recognize.

PART THREE

❧

Putting It All Together

CHAPTER TEN

Miracles in Action

*E*verything I've written doesn't mean squat unless it is *lived* and put into action. It is possible to understand the concepts in this book and in the Course, and even teach them, but still have tricky areas in your life that are ruled by ego. For instance, the ego is happy to "be spiritual" and "choose love" by itself, thus trying to solve its problems without our Inner Therapist's help. This keeps real Love at bay because unconscious fears remain intact and un-examined.

In this chapter and the next, I share some common anxiety-laden situations and show how I worked through them using the principles I've described. If you've dealt with chronic or recurring anxiety in your life, some of this may sound familiar.

Releasing Hypochondria and Worry about Your Body

My biggest anxiety triggers have been bodily concerns. I used to be an expert at freaking myself out over physical symptoms, and I went through cycles of health worries. If I noticed a physical symptom, I Googled it and decided it must be an early sign of an aneurysm, bird flu, cancer, diabetes, an *E. coli* infection, or something else. I could literally go through the whole alphabet. The incessant worry created more symptoms. Finally, I would go to a doctor, walk away with a clean bill of health, and discover that all the symptoms disappeared.

At times, when a doctor decided that one of my symptoms warranted further investigation, I experienced uncontrollable terror. My anxiety felt like a persecutor, as if it could grab me by the hair and shove my face into evidence that I was most certainly dying of a horrible disease.

Hypochondria. Debilitating? Yes. Deadly? No. If this pattern is familiar to you, here are some techniques to facilitate your journey from anxiety to love.

Bring Awareness to the Pattern

Write down your fear pattern as best you can, and better yet, start to label it when it's happening. Know that you are worrying right now. Know that you can create symptoms just by focusing on them. Know that there are other possible explanations for the symptoms you're feeling. Know that this is a learned worry pattern, and it is not permanent. One of the greatest gifts we have in the world is change, until the time comes when we remember Love, which is changeless.

Start Noticing the Subtle Voice of Fear

Notice that voice! And when you hear it, ask for a miracle from your Inner Therapist. When I was suffering from hypochondria,

I could often achieve a state of relative calm by working through the principles in this book. But then I might feel a mild sensation in my abdomen and hear a fearful whisper in my mind, such as "It's your liver." When I noticed the fear, I could either focus on it and fuel the fear or decide that I was ready to listen to my Inner Therapist *more* than to the fear.

If I felt I had no choice but to focus on the fear, I tried to acknowledge that there is a part of my mind that badly wants to think those obsessive thoughts because they prove to me that I am a body (see the section on unwillingness in chapter 7, step 6). If the fear feels irresistible, try the next step here.

Begin Releasing Everything

Revisit chapter 6, steps 3 and 5. One reason that health fears can have us in a headlock is that we're afraid of sickness, suffering, death, or separation from family. Write down every fear you can think of and ask your Inner Therapist for help in seeing them differently. If you are worrying about different body parts, name those specific parts. Place your heart, your brain, your lungs, your entire body, and everything you hold dear into your Inner Therapist's loving arms. There is where your safety truly lies, not in the world's hands. And when you sense hesitation or fear to release something, simply look at that hesitation with your Inner Therapist as well.

Go to the Doctor with Your Inner Therapist If You Need To

Do not feel guilty about going to the doctor. Whether or not you go really isn't the issue. It's not necessarily "spiritual" to keep trusting that all will be well because you think you *should* trust when you really don't. That's the ego trying to be spiritual. Do what you feel inclined to do (such as keeping a medical appointment), but do it with your Inner Therapist. Your willingness is what is important. When you go to the doctor, are you willing to go with your Inner Therapist in mind? Are you willing to follow through with that choice? Are you willing to not listen to the ego's shrieks of fear and instead turn to your Inner Therapist, regardless of the external circumstances? Be a happy learner. As you allow your fears to be transformed and transfer your trust to your Inner Therapist instead of to the ego, you'll always know the best course of action to take.

And if you're not going to the doctor because you're terrified of medical appointments, know that when you go, it will give you an opportunity to practice facing fear with your Inner Therapist. You never have to face fear alone. Even if you're terrified, there's a quiet witness in your mind, evidence of your split mind, that is waiting for you to listen (revisit my story about blood tests in chapter 6, step 4). If you can learn a lesson without going to the doctor, the urge to go and the fear of going will fall away.

Notice the Quiet Presence in Your Mind Standing for Love

When you experience fear in any form, remember that it is because you are misperceiving and seeing through the lens of the ego rather than with the vision of your Inner Therapist. Remember that the body's eyes report only separation to you. Miracles restore our perception from wrong-mindedness to right-mindedness. Ask your Inner Therapist for a miracle instead.

Through that miracle, you can begin to see that even when you're fixated on fear, there is still a quiet place of Love in your mind, attesting to the fact that what you truly are cannot be harmed and that you can wake up to this realization now. This quiet place of Love in your mind is waiting for you to pay attention to it so that your awareness of it can grow.

Be Willing to Focus on Love and to Get Quiet

Instead of fixating on ideas like "Oh my gosh, what's wrong with me, and how much will I suffer?," we have to *want* to focus on a new possibility of inner peace and knowing Love. This may seem impossible, because we cannot sense how near it is. But "this love-liness is not a fantasy. It is the real world, bright and clean and new, with everything sparkling under the open sun. Nothing is hidden here, for everything has been forgiven and there are no fantasies to hide the truth" (ACIM T-17.II.2:1–3).

Be willing to focus on Love (rather than fixate on the habit of fear). And then grab your meditation cushion. It's time to get quiet. Give every fear that arises to your Inner Therapist and, with a heartfelt desire, ask for a miracle instead of fear. Your body is a learning device for your mind. So whenever something seems not right with your body — a stab of pain, a strange sensation, a worrisome symptom — give it to the one true physician, your Inner Therapist, asking that your *perceptions* of the body be healed. Our Inner Therapist is the only physician who can really heal, because it is the mind, which believes in separation, that needs healing, not the body. The body's symptoms and sensations are really just effects of the mind's projections. Revisit the "Releasing Worry about Your Body" meditation in chapter 8, shift 4.

Passing through Panic Attacks

My panic attacks used to happen spontaneously during the day, they woke me up at night, and sometimes they lasted two weeks at a time. The dry heaves, stomach spasms, and trouble eating were "evidence" from the ego that I was losing my mind to anxiety. But I refused to lose hope of recovery.

Extreme suffering brings you to your knees, and this is a great time to start letting go. Being in a state of relinquishment is actually a good place to be. If you're stuck in panic mode, let the anxiety crack you open to release even more to your Inner Therapist than you thought you could. Revisit the "laundry list" exercises in chapter 6, steps 3 and 5. In relinquishing a thought system that doesn't work and exchanging it for a new thought system of peace, all you have to lose is fear.

My stepfather once said something that made me feel renewed hope. He told me, "The light in you is too bright to fail." When he looked at me, I could see that he refused to believe in the sorry picture of his stepdaughter curled up on his couch, dark circles under her eyes, unable to eat, trembling uncontrollably. He refused to believe it because he sided with our Inner Therapist's vision. And that was exactly the help I needed at that moment.

I say it now to you: "The light in *you* is too bright to fail."

When anxiety kicks up, you have a number of options, but ultimately, the only way through it is through it. And going through it looks different every time, for everyone.

Options for Intense Times

In the midst of an anxiety episode, you have to decide the right way for you to handle it. Here are some options, listed in no particular order:

1. *Review the mind-straightening mantras or perception shifts that give you hope that you will make it through this.* You *will* make it through, even if you are feeling stuck in your anxiety pattern. When you are willing to listen to the Inner Therapist instead of the ego, "success in transcending the ego is guaranteed"

(ACIM T-8.V.4:4). Practice the mind-straightening mantras and antianxiety meditations as well as you can right now.

2. *See if you can work on accepting (or at least acknowledging) that anxiety is happening right now.* We want it to go away so badly that just accepting it for what it is can seem impossible. Remember, this is happening because it is an opportunity for you to grow and learn. Be open to what you can learn from the anxiety.

3. *Turn to an earthly therapist for help.* Many counseling techniques can help you deal with anxiety. Your therapist should be part of your circle of support: if you don't feel comfortable with your therapist, find a different one. Remember, our Inner Therapist can sometimes speak through others when we're too stricken by fear to hear it in ourselves.

4. *Consider medication.* When I was experiencing intense panic, medication was the only thing that brought relief. The fear had such a strong hold that I needed external help to loosen its grip. For me, medication was like the eye of a hurricane. It gave me a break and some breathing room before I faced the rest of the storm. There is nothing wrong with this option, and no reason to feel guilt. Be willing to take the medication (whether it's pharmaceuticals or "natural" remedies) with your Inner Therapist rather than with the ego. It may not be fixing the root of the problem, but you're still working on that root (the unconscious guilt we carry) while experiencing some temporary relief. If you take your medication with the Inner

Therapist, you'll stop needing it when you are ready to let go of that guilt.

5. *Try temporary distraction.* Sometimes distracting yourself helps reduce the intensity of the anxiety. I'm talking about healthy distractions, such as going for a walk — not alcohol or recreational drugs, which can simply add additional layers of fear to be undone. We have to be careful about using distractions, because we can fall into perpetual distraction as a way of avoiding dealing with the anxiety. Reserve distraction for the times when the anxiety feels too intense, and be willing to look at your distractions with your Inner Therapist.

6. *Look at what is arising inside you with your Inner Therapist, even if it is only for a moment.* If we feel we can't turn toward the anxiety on our own because it is too much, we can still be willing to look at the anxiety for just a moment with our Inner Therapist's help. I used to wake up with a ton of anxiety and jump out of bed to distract myself from it. Slowly, as I felt ready, I began to take a few moments on waking to look at what I was feeling with my Inner Therapist. This helped the anxiety fall away because I began to lose my fear of it.

7. *Remember your rock.* This is your support system and those people (or that one person) who are willing to look past the surface to the truth. You are well. You are not sick. You are not a body. Love is who you are.

8. *Meditate.* The following meditation can help you move through and out of anxiety.

LET'S MEDITATE: PASSING THROUGH ANXIETY

Grounding with the breath, sense it going in and out. You can always come back to this breath if you need to orient yourself to the present.

Acknowledge that anxiety is present. Notice whether you are breathing from high up in your chest. If you are, soften your abdominal muscles to allow your belly to expand and contract as you breathe.

Say to yourself: "The light in me is too bright to fail. If I am experiencing lack of peace in any form, I am simply misperceiving, that is all. I am not going crazy; I am learning to become more sane."

Visualize the anxiety as a heavy fog over your mind. Anxiety can exist only in time, not in truth, and it will pass. It is just a fog, a simple misperception. It has no power to hurt you.

As you breathe in and out, imagine seeing the fog passing by. It has no power to change the truth about you. A deep part of you is always at peace, even though the surface part may be focused on the fog of fear or pain.

Noticing your breath, imagine yourself dropping beneath the fog, gently resting as it floats by overhead. As you breathe and rest beneath the fog, you reconnect with the part of your mind that is always at peace.

Now connect with your willingness to see the fog differently. Imagine that your willingness is the sun that burns away the fog. You see that the fog has no power over you — it is not who you are. You are peace, and joy, and love.

Say to yourself, "Peace is what I am, and I am willing to claim it now."

Moving through Anxiety Based on External Events

The secret of salvation is but this:
that you are doing this unto to yourself.

ACIM T-27.VIII.10:1

Recently, my beautiful husband was participating in a lifeguard boat relay at the beach. Although it was a gorgeous evening, big waves were breaking directly on the sand. As my husband stood in the shallow water preparing to take his turn racing the boat, I watched in horror as a massive wave caught the seventeen-foot wooden boat, hurling it sideways and out of control. The rowers in the boat jumped out to protect themselves. The boat shot at my husband like a rocket. Standing in shallow and turbulent seawater, he threw his body backward to duck under the boat, whose keel passed only inches above his head. The water was so shallow that had he been wearing a helmet as I had always wanted him to, the bottom of the boat would probably have snagged the brim of the helmet and injured him.

I was flooded with fear. Trembling, I couldn't hold back my tears. My whole life with my husband flashed before me.

Later, as we were leaving the beach in subdued silence, a passerby said to my husband, "Your angels were with you today. You had only just enough water to get your head and body under that boat!"

My emotions were overwhelming and conflicting. I felt gratitude that he was okay, fury that the event hadn't been canceled because of the waves, and anger at my husband for participating in these competitions. I withdrew from him. Usually expressive and comfortable with my feelings, I felt numb and speechless. He got the coldest of shoulders.

Let me tell you, even though this world is an illusion, this incident certainly felt very real! I was so angry and upset that I went mute for twenty-four hours.

We were very fortunate that my husband was not hurt. But when terrible events happen in the world, they usually violate every law we expect to hold true. And it is through feeling that our world has been turned upside down that we are hurled into remembering that the world actually follows no laws that make sense. Under the ego's rule in the separation theme park, it can be a house of horrors.

Yet our Inner Therapist has a different interpretation for every challenging situation and will use the occasion as a means for our awakening if we will let it. Our Inner Therapist never leads us into pain, loss, or sacrifice. Those experiences are derived only from the ego.

Because the Course is my operating system, I had to see this situation through the eyes of my Inner Therapist in order to move through it. But I wasn't ready to do that right away. Here are a few techniques I used after this incident to help me through. Consider using these when you are dealing with an external event that is causing you distress.

Feel Your Feelings

One of the healthiest things you can do for your spiritual development is to feel your feelings. You cannot stuff them away inside, suppress them, or skip over them. You must feel them. If you're anxious, feel it. If you're horrified, angry, or upset, feel it. Our feelings aren't always comfortable, but remember, radical honesty is required in the journey from anxiety to love. This honesty means you must feel what you're feeling, including how your body and this world feel very real to you. When you're ready, you can look at these feelings with your Inner Therapist.

Identify the Witness You Are Calling Forth

Everything that we see is an "outward picture" of an inward state of mind (ACIM T-24.VII.8:10). We're constantly calling forth witnesses to fear or witnesses to love. Witnesses to fear say, "Look! You should be afraid because you can be hurt, and you *are* a body!" Witnesses to love affirm that you are something much greater than a body.

Clearly, the situation with my husband and the boat was a witness to fear. But how was it coming from my mind? I didn't want that to be true, and I was not in charge of the waves, so how could this situation possibly have come from me?

I remember feeling a tiny willingness to play with the idea that maybe this whole occurrence was somehow a projection coming from me, although I had moments of fluctuation between angrily saying, "F—— this Course stuff!" and feeling willingness to look at this with my Inner Therapist.

Whatever your situation, consider whether it is a witness for fear or a witness for love. Chances are that if it's troubling you, it is a witness for fear. You have the power to allow this witness for fear to be repurposed by your Inner Therapist, so that it can instead become a witness for love and help you remember that you're not a body.

Where Is the Blame?

When something unexpected happens, especially something unwanted, it's a natural reaction to want to blame someone else. Their guilt establishes our innocence. It is true that people can act insanely in this world and choose to do horrible things. They have a responsibility for their actions, which they may or may not accept. Yet we have a responsibility, too, in any given situation. Are we going to keep the blame and guilt in place, which is what the ego would prefer, or are we willing to see the situation through the Inner Therapist's eyes? We have to decide whether we want to stay with blame or move into willingness. It is okay if we are not willing to see through our Inner Therapist's eyes right now. If that's the case, we can be willing to look at the urge to blame with our Inner Therapist. This can actually be quite revealing.

I was intensely angry at my husband for putting me through such a frightening experience. I allowed myself to feel these feelings. Yet I also questioned why I was feeling so much rage even though he was okay. As I felt willingness to look at this situation with my Inner Therapist, this thought came forth: the raging anger I felt showed me that I'm still attached to my identity in this world. A deep part of me feels guilty about my investment in the world, and I felt anger because I prefer to keep this guilt hidden. If that's not something to take to my Inner Therapist, then I don't know what is!

Even Though This Feels Very Real, It Isn't the Truth, Because It Isn't Love

In order to see with our Inner Therapist's vision, we have to practice the "proper use of denial" (ACIM T-2.II.1:12). The body's eyes always report evidence of separation to us. To see with a new set of eyes, we have to remind ourselves that what we are experiencing feels very real but isn't the truth. The form isn't the truth. Death isn't the truth. Sickness and suffering are not the truth. Deny that the experience is real, and give it to your Inner Therapist. When we deny what we see, we are essentially saying that what is "out there" is an effect of our sleeping Child Mind and *cannot* change the truth about ourselves or anyone else. Try out lesson 14 from the Course:

> With eyes closed, think of all the horrors in the world that cross your mind. Name each one as it occurs to you, and then deny its reality. God did not create it, and so it is not real. Say, for example:

God did not create that war, and so it is not real.

God did not create that airplane crash, and so it is not real.

God did not create that disaster [*specify*], and so it is not real.

Suitable subjects for the application of today's idea also include anything you are afraid might happen to you or to anyone about whom you are concerned. In each case, name the "disaster" quite specifically. Do not use general terms. For example, do not say, "God did not create illness," but, "God did not create cancer," or heart attacks, or whatever may arouse fear in you.

This is your personal repertory of horrors at which you are looking. These things are part of the world you see. Some of them are shared illusions, and others are part of your personal hell. It does not matter. What God did not create can only be in your own mind apart from His. Therefore, it has no meaning. In recognition of this fact, conclude the practice periods by repeating today's idea:

God did not create a meaningless world. (ACIM W-pI.14.4–6)

When you are done practicing this lesson, you can imagine giving the things you deny to your Inner Therapist. We cannot deny these things by ourselves, because we *do* believe these things are real. We always need the help of our Inner Therapist, which is outside our ego thought system.

Remember That You Are Here to Be a Miracle Worker

Whatever you experience in this ego world, your responsibility is always the same: to allow the undoing of fear in your own mind in order for your awareness of Love to be restored. This enables you to express the Love that you are made of, which re-awakens others to the Love within them, which in turn reinforces it in yourself. This all comes down to your willingness to give what you experience to your Inner Therapist in exchange for a miracle.

When I finally decided that I was ready for a shift, I was willing to see that what I saw at the beach was part of a dream, and I was ready to look beyond it. My ego identity (Corinne) and my husband's ego identity (Rob) are both part of the illusion. What we all are in truth cannot be hurt, bruised, or broken, and what we are cannot die. I am not a body. I want to see with the vision of the Inner Therapist. I am willing. And so the shift came.

After twenty-four hours of not speaking, I sat in my backyard and was overwhelmed with a feeling of peace inside. When my husband came home from work that day, I greeted him with a smile rather than with tears.

I could have used this incident as justification to demand that my husband never participate in a boat relay again (solidifying the belief in my mind that this world is scary and that loss is real). This would have created tension with my husband, who loves these events. Instead, through willingness, my Inner Therapist used this situation to remind me that I am dreaming this dream and that there is nothing to be afraid of, because I am not Corinne. Not only did peace return to me and to my husband (who was very distressed that I was mad at him), but the love between us felt boundless and eternal as a result of the miracle I experienced. It was a love based on abundance, not on fear of loss.

To experience a miracle, embrace your willingness, hand it over, and get quiet. Try the following meditation to help.

LET'S MEDITATE:
DROPPING BENEATH YOUR PROBLEM

This is a meditation for taking a break from anxiety about something that is still happening, or for when you feel stuck on a particular problem.

Begin by noticing that you're obsessing over something. Visualize your problem as having a specific shape and color. For example, it might take the shape of an unruly ball of twine.

Imagine dropping beneath that unruly problem with Love by your side, quietly watching the chaos pass by overhead.

Beyond the perceived problem is a quiet, still space in you, which remains unchanged despite whatever seems to confront you. This is the place where we are going to rest, in stillness and trust.

While pausing in the stillness, stay connected to your willingness to see the problem differently as you rest outside this chaotic energy.

Notice what it feels like to be separate from your problem. Be the quiet observer. Be at ease, and take a break from trying to solve the problem. Notice that it feels good: you might notice calmness, or a renewed sense of trust that things will work themselves out.

You don't have to participate in the chaos. You can quietly witness it all unfolding without feeling involved.

Trust that things will shift when they are ready to shift, or that your next step to take will be made clear.

Continue to rest in this quiet space for as long as you'd like.

CHAPTER ELEVEN

More Miracles in Action

ᕙᕗ

*E*ach of these stories demonstrates that no matter what the situation, the goal of healing is always the same: to remember the truth about ourselves. It has never changed: we just haven't accepted it yet. We can only remember this truth through our Inner Therapist, and as we remember it, anxiety falls away. The following stories are additional anxiety scenarios, with tools for you to work through them.

Peace in a Crowd:
Finding Freedom from Social Anxiety

I was at a social gathering recently with a group with whom I don't have much in common. I felt that none of the people there understood my spiritual work or shared other interests with me.

While getting ready for the gathering, I noticed the usual feeling in the pit of my stomach telling me I wouldn't fit in. I also noticed feeling pressured to look a certain way (for instance, I feared my unpainted toenails might be judged as gross). Fears of being judged for bare toenails took over, so I painted on some funky royal-blue nail polish. (How insane is fear?)

Social anxiety is a wonderful demonstration of our belief in separation. We feel anxious being with others because we wholeheartedly believe they are separate from us, have the power to make us feel excluded, and are capable of hurting us with their judgment. Yet who is actually doing the judging?

Notice Your Judgments

As I reflected on my situation, I wondered, who is judging first? Is it them, or is it me? I'm willing to look, and I hope you are, too!

I'd like to think that it is other people who are judging. "They" are the ones judging "me" and causing me to feel self-conscious. This keeps me separate from them and unable to do anything about it except judge them or avoid the situation. In this way, I'm keeping the ego alive and well. I am holding them to their ego identities, and I'm holding to my own ego identity. I'm also telling myself that something outside me is causing me to feel the way I do.

However, much to the ego's dismay, I recognize that I am actually being the first one to judge. I'm judging in many ways: that "they" should be different than they are, that "they" are something separate from me. At a deep level, I am judging them as separate from me because I want to stay in this dream of separation. I "hired" them to help me keep the separation going. In addition, I am harshly judging myself as not worthy, an outsider, and different.

The entire time I was at this party, I completely forgot about my Inner Therapist! I thought about it before and after the party, but not while I was sucked into self-conscious mode.

Use the Anxiety Barometer

Feeling self-conscious is an ego alert! Self-consciousness means you're conscious of yourself — that is, the small-s ego self.

Self-consciousness is the perfect ego ploy to keep you believing that you're limited to a personality with a body. It is also a perfect barometer for indicating who you are siding with. If you're siding with the ego, self-consciousness feels strong. If you're siding with your Inner Therapist (and therefore are conscious of your Self), you feel peace.

When you notice that self-consciousness is strong, revisit the "Reading Your Anxiety Barometer" activity in chapter 4. It will help you shift into siding with your capital-S Self rather than the small-s ego self.

Get Radically Honest

I realized that I need to be brutally honest about the thoughts that go through my mind in uncomfortable social situations — including the fleeting "scraps of fear" (ACIM T-4.III.7:2) and my judgments of others or myself. If I can acknowledge that those thoughts are there, I can decide to bring them out of the shadows and into the light of healing by looking at them with my Inner Therapist. Some of my fearful and judgmental thoughts were these:

- I am afraid they are going to judge me.
- I am afraid of not fitting in and being rejected.
- I am too quiet.
- I am not funny enough.

- I am more spiritual than they are.
- They care too much about material things of this world, so they are less than me.
- I have to dress up to make myself feel like I will be accepted and equal to, if not better than, them.

These judgmental thoughts clearly reflect a belief that I can be attacked (by their judgments) and attack myself (by my own self-criticism) and that I can attack others (by judging them as inferior). All attack is Self-attack, meaning that I am actively working to keep Love out of my awareness and thus maintain my separateness from them. I must look at my belief in attack with my Inner Therapist in order to undo it and restore my awareness of Love.

Make a list of the thoughts that go through your mind in uncomfortable social situations. Write down your fears and your judgment of yourself and others. Be honest! You might be surprised at the judgments that are hiding out, not wanting to be seen. After you make your list, consider whether these thoughts may reflect a belief that you can attack and be attacked. Love is incapable of attacking or being attacked. So be willing to look at each judgment, *without judgment*, with your Inner Therapist in order to release these beliefs. Slowly look at each thought and say, "Inner Therapist, I'm willing to bring this to the light to be healed. Please look at it with me."

Remember Your Worth

It is also important to recognize your true worth if you are struggling with feelings of inadequacy. One helpful teaching from the Course is that you cannot change your worth because it has already been established:

Your worth is not established by teaching or learning.
Your worth is established by God....

Again,—nothing you do or think or wish or make is
necessary to establish your worth. (ACIM T-4.I.7:1,2,6)

You are wholly worthy. The ego will tell you otherwise, but
you are learning by now that you are not the ego. If you feel discomfort in any form, it means that you are simply misperceiving,
and so it becomes an opportunity to choose again. Does this mean
that you need to stay in situations where you are uncomfortable?
Certainly not. But "discomfort is aroused only to bring the need
for correction into awareness" (ACIM T-2.V.7:8). So if you are
experiencing discomfort, it becomes an opportunity to look with
your Inner Therapist at what is coming up. That's all we have to
do: give our willingness to our Inner Therapist and ask for it to be
exchanged for the miracle instead.

Remember You Cannot Be Rejected

If you ever struggle with fears of abandonment or rejection,
remember that you have not separated from Love. Your Loving Source is not outside you, and you belong to Love, forever.
Quite literally, "God goes with you wherever you go" (ACIM
W-pI.41.4:4). If others seem to reject you, they are giving you an
opportunity to look with your Inner Therapist at what is coming
up. Revisit the laundry-list exercise in chapter 6, steps 3 and 5, and
include your fear of rejection in the exercise. Your Inner Therapist and Love itself will never leave you. As you come to know
this truth, fears of rejection fade, and you become comfortable
with who you are.

LET'S MEDITATE: RELEASING SOCIAL ANXIETY

This meditation is for anytime you anticipate being in an uncomfortable social situation.

Begin by taking a few mindful breaths in and out, releasing any tightness and allowing the breath to flow freely to and from the belly. The breath is our anchor to this present moment, so if you find your attention wandering, simply bring your attention back to the sensation of the breath.

Notice what kind of fears come up about the social situation. Do you fear being judged or embarrassed, or simply not knowing what to say? Notice any tension forming in the body as you think about this.

Noting the fear, say to your Inner Therapist, "I am willing to see this social situation differently. I am willing to see that *they* are not making me anxious, but that the ego is just telling me they are separate from me." Imagine giving your fear to your Inner Therapist, and say, "I want a miracle instead."

Whatever the form of the fear, know that it is just the ego offering you a "gift" of anxiety, hoping you will stay identified with your small-s self.

Say to yourself, "May the light in me join with the light in others. There is nothing to fear."

"I would like to call forth witnesses in this social situation that show me that I am love."

"Nothing that I think, do, or say can establish my worth. My worth is established by God."

As you feel the truth of these words, place your

thumb, index finger, and middle finger together. This is a reminder in the form of physical touch that you can use whenever you begin to feel anxious. Allow the three fingers touching to remind you that you are not alone; Love is always by your side. Allow the three fingers to remind you to breathe. There is nothing to fear. Allow the three fingers to remind you that your worth is established by God. Nothing can change that.

Continue to rest in trust as you relax with this reminder. When you are ready, release your fingers.

Whenever you are anxious in a social situation, you can put your three fingers together as a reminder that there is nothing to fear.

Caring with Love Instead of Fear: Working through Worry about Another Person

In this world it is very natural to worry about our loved ones. We don't want them to be hurt or to suffer in any way. Yet what if this worry is somehow hurting instead of helping?

For years my mom has struggled with severe migraines. One night I was lying in bed thinking about her and how it upsets me to think that she is in pain. I love her so much and want her to be safe and protected. Then I had a stunning realization: that feeling protective of her body, wanting her to get medical help, and worrying about her physical state are all forms of attack (not real love). By worrying about her body, I am saying that she is limited to a body and reinforcing the belief that she can be hurt. I love her and want to save and protect her, but in worrying about her body I am attacking her. It is fear masked as love. Whoa!

Find Your Willingness... Again!

I immediately recognized that I don't want to keep any fear or attack thoughts because I want to be truly helpful. Otherwise I am reinforcing the error in both our minds, rather than bringing it to the light to be undone. I do not know, however, how not to see my mom as a body. Here again is the importance of willingness!

Revisit chapter 6, step 1, if you need a willingness boost. Find your willingness to see the person you are worrying about differently, to come to know who you both really are, and give it to your Inner Therapist.

Use Your Inner Therapist's Vision Instead of Your Own

If I decide by myself that I'm not going to believe in my mom's illness, that is going to come across as denial and may not provide the compassion she may need. It is also a form of "level confusion" (ACIM T-2.IV.2:2), meaning that I am taking on the Inner Therapist's job of looking past the illusion by myself, even though I still believe in it.

Always be willing to use your Inner Therapist's vision instead of your own. The body's eyes deceive. As you side with your Inner Therapist's vision, you align your mind with the Love in the other person, thus reinforcing it in yourself. Your Inner Therapist sees only what is true, which can result in healing for both you and the other person.

Use True Empathy

There is a difference between the ego's use of empathy and "true empathy" (ACIM T-16.I). To the ego, to feel empathy means to pity and feel really bad for someone else. For example, when my mom is hurting, I'm hurting. I'm completely identified with her pain, not with her truth and light. Joining in suffering means we're holding ourselves and the other person to the pain of the ego and actually are not allowing healing Love in.

Here is the alternative to the ego's use of empathy. When my mom is hurting, I notice empathy arising in me, and I give my capacity for empathy to my Inner Therapist. I ask that my capacity for empathy be used for healing and for awakening, rather than reinforcing the belief that we are separate bodies:

> The capacity to empathize is very useful to the Holy Spirit, provided you let Him use it in His way. His way is very different. He does not understand suffering, and would have you teach it is not understandable. When He relates through you, He does not relate through your ego to another ego. He does not join in pain, understanding that healing pain is not accomplished by delusional attempts to enter into it, and lighten it by sharing the delusion. (ACIM T-16.I.1:3–7)

To use true empathy, notice when empathy and worry arise, give your capacity for empathy and worry to your Inner Therapist, and be willing to see only what is true in the other person, which is Love. The ego in you can only join with the ego in another. But when you are willing to side with your Inner Therapist, the Love in you joins with the Love in another, and you are both healed as a result. This reinforces your experiential knowing that your Inner Therapist is really there, and that you and the other person are not bodies. "Yet of this you may be sure; if you will merely sit quietly by and let the Holy Spirit relate through you, you will empathize with strength, and will gain in strength and not in weakness" (ACIM T-16.I.2:7).

This is how you can heal others. Love them so much that you are willing to allow your own mind to be healed. The next two stories illustrate how accepting the undoing of fear in our minds can touch others without your saying a word to them. But first, grab that meditation cushion.

LET'S MEDITATE: FINDING A NEW PERCEPTION WHEN WORRYING ABOUT SOMEONE ELSE

When you are caught up in worrying about another person, this meditation can help. Just as we practiced in the rock meditation from chapter 9, healing can happen when we see through the eyes of our Inner Therapist instead of the body's eyes.

Begin by taking a few mindful breaths, in and out, noticing the rise and fall of the belly as you breathe. The breath is our anchor to this present moment, so if you find your mind wandering, simply bring it back to the sensation of the breath.

Drop into your feeling of care for this person, noticing the loving feelings that flow from your heart. Say to yourself, "I can be most helpful if I am willing to see the truth in another, rather than siding with fear.

"If I am seeing suffering of any kind, I've chosen to listen to the voice of separation. To see the truth in this other person, I need healing for my own mind.

"Regardless of the situation that this person is dealing with, the truth remains unchanged. He or she is already perfect."

Turn to your Inner Therapist within and say, "Help me see only the truth. Help me focus on the fact that this person is already healed. I care so much that I am willing to allow my own mind to be healed with a new perception. I am willing to release my perception of their body and have it be replaced by a perception of their true wholeness. I am willing to side with the truth."

Take a few deep breaths as you conclude your meditation.

Getting Past Grievances with
Those Who Drive You Crazy

If you look closely and with radical honesty, you can probably list a number of grievances you hold toward people in your life. Your partner doesn't wash dishes the "right" way, your parent talks too much (or too little), or you still feel anger toward a friend for poking fun at you five years ago. Grievances can be subtle, but they have the power to keep you from remembering Love, and so they can keep you in anxiety.

When another person triggers a grievance in you, it is a chance to look at what it is bringing up in your mind. Through willingness, radical honesty, and turning to your Inner Therapist, you may bring about a miracle not just for yourself but for everyone involved.

I was once very angry with a friend and let her know it. I felt she was making a mistake in handling her money that reflected a negative pattern she has followed as long as I can remember. I wanted my friend to turn to her Inner Therapist like I do, dammit, and I tried to convince her that she should give that a try, even though she had no interest in the Course or spirituality. Although I was mostly aware of feeling anger, beneath it was fear. I was terribly scared that my friend would suffer because of her decision, and I hated seeing her overwhelmed and constantly stressed out. I was angry and annoyed for several days, but eventually I felt a willingness to see the situation differently. I realized I did not trust her to make the right decision.

Through turning to my Inner Therapist, this thought came forward: "I don't have to trust her at all: I trust the Inner Therapist within her." Bingo! That was all I had to do. Whatever choices she made, I could trust that the Inner Therapist was in her mind. Whether or not she chose to listen was her decision.

When you feel that someone else is "causing" your lack of peace, it's time for *you* to choose a miracle. That person is stirring up your stuff because it is an opportunity for *both of you* to experience a healing. Trust the Inner Therapist, and be willing to release your attachment to the outcome of their behavior.

Let Other People Be as They Are

As you have learned the importance of allowing yourself to be where you are, can you extend this loving perspective to others? I gave my feeling of wanting my friend to do things differently to my Inner Therapist (remember, forgiveness means that any judgment I'm holding is *for giving* to my Inner Therapist). My friend was exactly where she needed to be for her own growth and learning, and I am always exactly where I need to be for mine. I'd tried to correct her many times, only to learn that it didn't work. I could let her be where she was only because I could allow myself to be where I was.

Instantly I felt a rush of love, and my peace returned. I felt moved to send my friend a simple email, saying, "I love you and I treasure our friendship." She told me that was exactly what she needed to hear, and it shifted her out of her stressful state.

Drop the Desire to Attack

When you're triggered, ask yourself this question, "Am I willing to drop the desire to attack?" You don't have to actually do it: you just have to be *willing* to. I've learned that when I lash out, all that happens is that I feel guilty for making the other person feel guilty (which ultimately only hurts me). Get super clear about your intention. If there is a small part of you that isn't willing, simply look at that with your Inner Therapist.

Bring Your Attention to Your Inner Therapist

Regardless of what the other person is doing, be willing to bring your attention to your Inner Therapist. To avoid giving in to the desire to attack, it can be helpful to focus on something concrete and peaceful like a beautiful photo, the sky, your backyard, or a flower, while keeping your Inner Therapist in mind.

A few days after I sent the email expressing my feelings about our friendship, I was on the phone with my friend. When she began describing her elaborate plan to "save" herself financially, I felt a familiar twinge of annoyance. But rather than get angry at her again, I remembered that I was willing to trust that the Inner Therapist is in her, period.

I stared up at the trees as I sat on my back porch, listening. Though I continued to listen to and understand her, my friend's words became neutral sounds and syllables. I felt myself feeling detached from the situation. It was as if I was being lifted "above the battleground" (ACIM T-23.IV). I felt willingness to be led past the picture, to see the truth behind the form. I did not feel the need to attack, I did not feel angry: instead I felt peace and love. For ten minutes while I listened to her, I felt the willingness to see with the Inner Therapist's vision. It occurred to me that the Inner Therapist sees all our shenanigans but looks straight past them to the truth beyond.

Believe in the Miracles When They Happen

As I listened without judgment to my friend, she suddenly made an astonishing remark. She told me about her realization that the thrill she felt about a business success was an ego reaction. "I never thought I had an ego, and I do," she said.

Suddenly my friend was recognizing her ego pattern! I'd never heard her do so before. I smiled, feeling that this was an external validation of my turning toward my Inner Therapist. But I knew that I had not made this change come about in my friend; all I did was muster the willingness to get my own ego out of the way and trust the Inner Therapist in another person.

When things like this happen, pay attention to them. There are no accidents or coincidences. Your inner decision may lead to a shift in outside circumstances. These experiences serve as cornerstones that support our new foundation built on Love, a much more stable home than the ego's unstable structure, built on fear, judgment, and grievances.

Getting through Medical Testing: Finding Peace Regardless of the Outcome

Having to go through medical testing for potentially serious health problems is scary, whether or not you have chronic anxiety. As you know by now, one of the ego's favorite ways to hook my attention has been through fear of sickness. For most of my life, I've followed a pattern of focusing on physical symptoms and worshipping the "god of sickness" (ACIM T-10.III.9:4) (which the Course says is really a belief in nothing).

I recently had a wonderful opportunity to look at my firm belief my body can hurt me. I've always avoided uncertainty surrounding health concerns, rushing to the doctor at the first hint that something might be wrong with my body. Suspecting trouble but not having answers was a condition I avoided like the plague (pun intended).

To the unhappiness of my ego identity, I was recently in a state of uncertainty for several months. I had been undergoing a series of lab tests because one inconclusive but abnormal test result led to another. I also had a biopsy of something "unknown" that was removed from my body. I had moments of terror, but there were also moments where I was able to rest in pure innocence, feeling it was impossible for anything to hurt me.

Having had to wait for test results in the past, I was well aware that I had two choices: I could freak out, meaning that I would feel better only when (or if) I got a clean bill of health, or I could decide to look for my peace where I might actually find it.

Seek Peace That Does Not Depend on a Test Result

I decided that I wanted to find the type of peace that did not depend on a test result, and I became wholly willing to find it. This may sound impossible, especially if you are currently facing medical testing or illness. However, you have been learning all along that you are not your body and that the truth of who you are cannot be hurt. Those are not just words but truth. And we can come to know this truth through our own experience.

Every time I felt the fear of sickness arise and the strong pull to believe in it, I turned to my Inner Therapist, asking to be taught about the *un*importance of the body. The Course promises, "I can be entrusted with your body and your ego only because this enables you not to be concerned with them, and lets me teach you their unimportance" (ACIM T-4.I.13:4).

Ask yourself right now, "Am I willing to find the type of peace that does not depend on the outcome of a test result?" I'll bet you are.

Work with the Spikes of Fear Rather Than Running Away from Them

The anxiety I was experiencing was coming from the ego, because the ego knew it would be a hook with irresistible bait. *Not this time.*

When you feel spikes of fear, work with these three steps based on those in chapter 5.

Step 1. Every moment when any fear arises (from fear of death to fear of the flu), be willing to look at that fear with the Inner Therapist rather than turning away from it or minimizing it. Unshakable peace is found through facing our fears with willingness.

Try out these statements of willingness:

- I am willing to look at this with you.
- I am willing to look at the beliefs I hold that are bringing this fear about.
- I am willing to own that this is coming from my split mind, even if I don't understand how.

- I am willing to be taught that my body can't cause me to be sick.
- I am willing to learn the body is an effect of the mind, and that the body is completely neutral.

Step 2. Clean up shop, and toss *everything* (your willingness, your hopes, your fears, your attachments, and so on) into your Inner Therapist's hands. When the fear grows strong, rather than dismissing it, minimizing it, or just telling yourself that your body will be okay, experiment with letting go of everything. Trust that you can learn true healing with the help of your Inner Therapist. Above all, this involves looking with the Inner Therapist at another layer of the blocks you have built against Love and allowing them to be undone as you become willing to let them go.

Use these mind-straightening mantras:

- "Take this from me and look upon it, judging it for me" (ACIM T-19.IV.C.i.11:8).
- Teach me the right perception of my body.
- Teach me how to think like you.
- I withhold absolutely nothing from you. Take it all.

Step 3. Seek a moment of quiet. At times, I felt too much fear to be able to meditate. I found that kneeling in a prayer pose helped my practice, especially in step 2, going through my laundry list of attachments and giving everything to my Inner Therapist. This pose helped me remember that I was done with being the maker of my own dream and was ready to let the Inner Therapist take the lead. As I truly relinquished everything, all that remained were joyful quiet and pure peace.

Every single time I felt a spike of fear, I worked through these steps as if my life depended on it. By handing over my fixed false perceptions to my Inner Therapist, I started to experience small glimpses of pure joy and a feeling that nothing could hurt me.

Sickness began to seem utterly preposterous. The thought that I might have cancer or something else seriously wrong felt so far out of the realm of possibility that it was laughable.

That's when I got the call from the doctor's office that my biopsy had come back normal. "Corinne" was relieved, but my Self was untouched, knowing that any picture of the world would not change the truth of who I was, no matter what the outcome might have been. The ego cannot change reality. As I worked through the steps above and rested many times in a place of pure joy and innocence, my belief in sickness felt like it was going down the drain.

"When I Am Healed I Am Not Healed Alone" (ACIM W-pI.137)

The call from my doctor came at 5:30 PM. That same day, unknown to me, my mom, seventy-five miles away, found herself looking at the clock in her kitchen, noticing that it was 5:31 PM. She had been in the midst of a cluster-type migraine headache, the kind that can last five days. One minute before I received the phone call, she experienced a sensation that felt like sandbags being lifted off her shoulders, resulting in the almost instant dissipation of the headache. Though she had suffered frequent headaches for years, she was free of them for weeks after this experience.

This healing could not have happened because she was relieved about my news, because she didn't know it yet. She had been working through the Course as I had been, and we simply both met the conditions of peace at the same time through our shared desire to see with our Inner Therapist's vision. This is how healing happens.

My healing happened when I decided to stop chasing after the god of sickness, running to the doctor every time I noticed a physical symptom. This time, running to the doctor wasn't an option because I was forced to wait for test results. Instead, I ran to my Inner Therapist. And I was serious; I let go more deeply than I thought I could. The miracle that came was a healing for me and my mom.

I had the thought that "the god of sickness is loosening its hold on me," but I was given an immediate internal correction: "No! I am learning how to let go of the god of sickness."

Recognizing That Peace Is Not Dependent on External Circumstances

All fear is the same. It takes countless different forms, but it stems from our desire to be an independent golden goose, separate from God, ruler of our own little universe. When we realize that we're completely and utterly dependent on our Inner Therapist, the Holy Spirit, that's when we recognize that we have a power within us that far exceeds anything that could be given us in this world.

The process of healing can be boiled down to one simple statement: *withhold nothing from your Inner Therapist.* If you truly desire healing, your mind will heal. Don't be discouraged about bumps in the road. They are opportunities to practice allowing fear to be undone in your mind. Each challenge is another layer of the onion. There are never any setbacks: everything is as it should be. And there is no sacrifice: the only thing you lose is pain.

This process takes extreme patience. Reorienting your mind toward Love rather than ego is difficult. It means giving up the habit of being the small-s ego self. Every little effort counts. I believe in you. We're healing together. Every gain that I've made is a gain for you, and every gain that you make is a gain for me. My gains are yours, and yours are mine, because we are *one*. We're going to make it. The light in you is too bright to fail.

APPENDIX

Quick Q & A

What is *A Course in Miracles*?

A Course in Miracles is a psychological and spiritual curriculum consisting of three parts: the Text, the Workbook, and the Manual for Teachers. It is a complete course of spiritual awakening that guides the practitioner through unlearning fear and remembering the truth of our existence, which is eternity.

How do I interpret the source citations for the ACIM quotes that appear throughout the book?

Quotations are cited according to the annotation system followed by the publisher, the Foundation for Inner Peace. Each citation begins with a letter representing the part of the book being quoted: T (Text), W (Workbook), M (Manual for Teachers), or C (Clarification of Terms, which follows the Manual for Teachers). The letter is followed by a chapter number, workbook lesson number, or section number, and then by a paragraph number and a page number. For a thorough explanation of the annotation system, please visit the Foundation for A Course in Miracles website (Facim .org) and search for "annotation."

I have made every effort to cite quotations accurately. If any errors have been made, I ask for your forgiveness.

Can you define some of the terms you use in this book?

Child Mind: The perfect creation of God, which comprises many Children. Part of this Child Mind is awake and home in the Mind of God, and part of it is dreaming of the world of form.

Ego: The fearful belief that you are a separate self and want to remain a separate self. This is the small-s self.

Forgiveness: The process of turning to our Inner Therapist to help us see that what we think is happening is just a dream. Thus, everything that occurs is "for giving" or "for-the-giving" to our Inner Therapist.

God: Our Loving Source of Oneness; pure Love that is also wholly loving.

Inner Therapist: Also known as the Holy Spirit or Higher Mind, this is the part of your mind that has not forgotten the truth of who you are. It is your connection to remembering our Oneness.

Self: The capital-S Self is the real you that exists beyond your body.

Separation: The belief that we are separate from our Source (God).

Separation theme park: The world that the body's eyes see.

What should I make of the masculine pronouns used in *A Course in Miracles?*

> *A Course in Miracles* uses masculine pronouns to describe God and the Holy Spirit (i.e., our Inner Therapist). However, these masculine pronouns are gender-neutral in intent. If this usage rouses a reaction in you, be willing to look at your reaction with your Inner Therapist. The Holy Spirit and God exist beyond the concepts of male or female.

Why am I experiencing anxiety?

> Anxiety is the ego's best evidence that we are limited to a body. Anxiety hurts, so the ego knows it can easily capture our attention this way. Anxiety drowns out our awareness of Love, which the ego doesn't want us to pay attention to. Yet when it is given to our Inner Therapist, anxiety can be our biggest asset in healing, because anxiety sufferers are extremely skilled at recognizing fear.

Where does anxiety come from?

> The deepest cause of anxiety comes from the sleeping part of the Child Mind, which is terrified that it is going to be punished for dreaming a dream of separation. For more on where anxiety comes from, see chapter 4.

How do I make the anxiety stop?

> Consider your options and what feels right for you. If you're in the thick of anxiety, check out the section "Passing through Panic Attacks" in chapter 10. Ultimately, anxiety falls away as we learn who we truly are.

Can I ever find peace again?

> Yes! We are here to heal and to learn that we are truly
> happy when we identify with the Self that abides beyond
> our body.

What can I do about fearing sickness?

> A happy learner does not feel guilty about learning.
> Go to the doctor and get a checkup if you feel the need
> to, while being willing to look at this feeling of need
> with your Inner Therapist. Also, check out the section
> "Releasing Hypochondria and Worry about Your Body"
> in chapter 10.

I often worry about things in general. What can I do about this?

> Begin to practice mindful awareness by noticing when
> you are worrying. Practice catching worry thoughts, and
> be willing to look at them with your Inner Therapist.

Is the Course opposed to medication?

> No! This Course quote was very helpful to me when I
> needed to rely on medication for relief: "Sometimes the
> illness has a sufficiently strong hold over the mind to
> render a person temporarily inaccessible to the Atone-
> ment [the undoing of fear]. In this case, it may be wise
> to utilize a compromise approach to mind and body, in
> which something from the outside is temporarily given
> healing belief" (ACIM T-2.IV.4:5–6).
>
> In other words, if you need medicine, take medi-
> cine. Just be willing to look at your belief that you need
> it with your Inner Therapist.

How come it seems that I keep turning things over to my Inner Therapist but I still have anxiety?

> The feelings are still there because you likely still hold an unconscious fear of Love (which we all have — you're not alone!). We have not yet accepted that we are already healed. Try dropping into the idea that you were created perfect and remain so. You will come to recognize this as you accept more Love into your awareness. In the meantime, do your part by withholding nothing from your Inner Therapist. Practice getting quiet through meditation. Be patient. There are never setbacks, only opportunities to learn.

I keep asking for miracles and nothing happens. Am I failing?

> You are most certainly *not* failing. We are healed and home in Love *already*. We simply need to accept this. If you ask for a shift and nothing happens, have you already decided what the miracle should look like? Do you have an outcome in mind? Get clear on your expectations and be willing to release them to your Inner Therapist. Consider that you may also be feeling an unwillingness to heal. Revisit chapter 7, step 6, to explore this. Finally, consider whether you might be asking for a miracle to avoid something you don't want to deal with. It might be that it is time to go through your lesson by addressing what you need to address, while bringing the situation to your Inner Therapist. Revisit chapter 7, step 10, on being a happy learner.

I don't feel confident in my ability to listen to my Inner Therapist instead of my ego. How do I know which voice I'm listening to?

Tuning in to the guidance of your Inner Therapist takes practice. Revisit chapter 3 for some pointers. In the meantime, there is good news. You don't have to worry about figuring out which voice you are listening to. As long as you are willing to give *all* your inclinations to your Inner Therapist (even if you only remember to do this after you have taken an action), you can be certain that ego will gently fall away when you are ready to let it go. We can't get this wrong!

What self-talk helped you with anxiety?

All of the mind-straightening mantras in the book helped me through anxiety. Use the ones that currently resonate with you, knowing that these may change frequently.

Are the meditations available as audio files?

To download three free meditations as audio files, visit FromAnxietyToLove.com/Meditations. The complete meditation album is also available for purchase at FromAnxietyToLove.com.

Acknowledgments

ᡣᢇᢓ

With so much gratitude...

To my dad, for your unending enthusiasm and support. I love you.

To my sweet "Buddha sister," for sharing this wonderful lifetime with me. I adore you.

To Betty and Bob, for playing a significant role in helping this book come to life and for believing in me every step of the way.

To my agent and editor, D. Patrick Miller, for seeing the potential in this project, for your talented editing, and for your sense of humor, which I appreciate so much.

To my New World Library family, for believing in this book as much as I do. And to Georgia Hughes, for saying yes to publishing this book, for your brilliant edits and fabulous feedback, and for being a joy to work with.

To Lorri Coburn, Julie Clayton, and Jessica Keet, for your edits and feedback on my manuscript, which played a significant role in its journey toward publication.

To my mom, for your edits and profound insights, which have enhanced this entire book. Your wisdom shines throughout these pages.

To Jon Mundy, for encouraging me to "keep writing."

To Carrie Triffet for your guidance and encouragement, to Amy Torres for your friendship, to Carole Christian for being a dear friend and mentor, and to Alan Cohen for your loving support.

To my counselor education crew at the College of New Jersey: Atsuko Seto, Jill Schwartz, Sandy Gibson, Stuart Roe, Mark Woodford, Marion Cavallaro, and Lisa Spencer. Stepping out of the scholarly realm and into spirituality was a scary professional step, and your loving support has meant more to me than you know.

To the participants on my Sunday night ACIM study-group calls. I love you all. And to Paula Shipman, Carol and Pat Corbett, Angela DiMarzo, Deedre Statz, and Paul LeBars, for being on our calls nearly every week for the past six years.

To my mighty companions and dear friends, Danielle Scruton and Craig Villarrubia, I can't imagine this journey without you.

To Nouk Sanchez, Coreen Walson, and John Mark Stroud, for playing significant roles in my healing journey. You have helped me take "the next step." Nouk, much of your wisdom is reflected throughout this book.

To Helen Schucman and Bill Thetford, for playing your role in bringing *A Course in Miracles* into the world. To Judy Skutch Whitson and Ken Wapnick, for your crucial roles in bringing the book into our hands, hearts, and minds.

To Robert Rosenthal, for a beautiful foreword and for your leadership in the Course community.

To the Foundation for Inner Peace, for allowing me to quote the Course throughout this book.

To Doug Thompson, for bringing us the Ur text. This deepened my experience of Love exponentially. I am forever grateful.

To Emily Bennington, for being a soul sister and introducing me to Robert Perry.

To Robert Perry, for your dedication to the Course and for reopening my eyes to what the Course actually says.

To my dearest friends, Jackie Pinkham, Amy Forsythe, Kelly Jackwicz, Kelly McClung, Beth Serughetti, Shawn Blue, Krystal Kavney, and Leah Winter, for always blowing me away with your love and support.

To Margaret Harsch Muchanic and Krista Muolo, for playing a role in my development of trust and experience of miracles without your even realizing it.

To Nicole Arioso, for your lifelong friendship. May we always have childlike fun together, especially on the beach and in the ocean.

To Aurora Myers and Allison Micco, for being fellow anxiety warriors and constantly inspiring me.

To Devi Kumar, Nadya Zhilaev, and my Hopewell crew, for giving me the opportunity each week to dive deep into mindfulness with you. It is truly an honor.

To you, the reader. Your decision to embark on this path helps strengthen these healing ideas in our collective mind. Thank you for the work you are doing. It helps all of us.

About the Author

Corinne Zupko was diagnosed with her first anxiety disorder at a very young age and struggled with debilitating anxiety for nearly three decades. Determined not to let the anxiety run her life, she has since become an expert in undoing anxiety through living the principles of the psychological and spiritual text *A Course in Miracles*. With the Course and mindfulness meditation as tools on her journey, she has found inner peace to be unstoppable and now teaches others to discover it in themselves.

Corinne has coached, counseled, and educated thousands of individuals at national and state conferences, in the classroom, in workshops, over the phone, and in the therapy chair. She holds an EdS degree in counseling with a concentration in meditation, an MA in counseling, and a BA in psychology. Corinne is a motivational and keynote speaker, a licensed professional counselor in the state of New Jersey, an adjunct professor of counselor education, a board-certified coach, and a teacher of Mindfulness-Based Stress Reduction. She teaches weekly mindfulness meditation classes at a major US financial institution. For more information, visit her website at FromAnxietyToLove.com.